INDIA

Photographs by

RAGHU RAI

Text by

USHA RAI

TIMES EDITIONS

This page: Sprucing up the outer walls of a temple is as important as keeping the sanctum sanctorium clean, particularly in a holy city like Hardwar where there are temples galore to attract the pilgrims. *Following pages:* Young girls participating in the Republic Day parade in New Delhi dress in the colorful costumes of Rajasthan and do the lezim, a folk dance;as the World Cup cricket series conclude at Calcutta's Eden Garden, fireworks illuminate the sky. Calcutta is a city where sports are taken seriously and, in India, special events such as this are often celebrated spectacularly.

Contents

India

A Land of Contrasts

On January 26 every year a sea of humanity descends on the sprawling green lawns of the Central Vista of Raj Path in India's capital, New Delhi, to witness the annual pageantry of the Republic Day parade.

They come in thousands, swathed in work-worn blankets to protect them from the chill January winds. All night long they trek to Raj Path and squat on either side of the parade road, huddled together for warmth. All castes and communities rub shoulders on this day — Brahmins and Sudras, Muslims, Jains, Hindus — as they wait patiently for the festivities to begin. As dawn breaks on fluttering flags and freshly painted lampposts, the excitement is palpably real.

This annual spectacle, graced by the President, the Prime Minister, visiting foreign dignitaries and the masses of India, is in microcosm what India is all about — its color and grandeur, its teeming masses, the amalgam of the traditional and the modern. It is part of India's exotic chemistry that the President should arrive for the parade in a ceremonial horse-drawn carriage of the colonial era while the Prime Minister with his phalanx of outriders arrives in a white indigenous bullet-proof Ambassador car.

The marching columns, the thundering and low-flying aircrafts reflect a modern, progressive India not too far behind the west in science and technology, developed within the country, while the colorful dancers, the traditional arts and crafts displayed on trundling floats boast of a heritage that is thousands of years old. The charm of India lies in the fact that it is a throbbing, living tradition that mingles harmoniously with the modern milieu.

Most visitors to India are shocked by the sheer numbers in the country. Over 850 million people. It is a secular country in the truest sense of the word, with several faiths, customs and beliefs and a babel of 17 recognized state languages and 541 dialects. Add to this the fact that each part of the country has its own customs, culture and cuisine and you wonder how these diverse people manage to communicate!

But it is precisely these vastly different people that make the country tick. If India works as a democracy, it is the people who make it so. They are curious, friendly to the

point of being intrusive, emotional and at all times they are colorful.

North Indians, particularly those from the states of Jammu and Kashmir, Punjab and Haryana, boasting of their Aryan lineage, are tall, wheat-complected and aggressive. Those of Punjab and Haryana are extremely hard-working, proving themselves to be the backbone of India's green revolution. By contrast the dark skinned Dravidians of the south — many of them almost negroid — are generally of a milder temperament. Arts and crafts, whether music, dance or sculpture, are in their blood. The women

*Tribals of Jhabua in Madhya Pradesh have their own way of celebrating Holi, the harvest festival (**left**), while in Hyderabad a statue of a dancing Nataraja outside a temple overlooks the 16th century Char Minar, a landmark of the city (**above**).*

from the south and east are petite, doe-eyed and with lustrous black hair — some almost flowing to the ankles, earning them a place in the Guiness Book of World Records.

Yet in this panoramic landscape of diverse languages, religions and cultures, there is a cohesiveness that spans 3,200 kilometers from Leh in the north to Kanyakumari in the south and 3,000 kilometers from Nagaland in the east to the Rann of Kutch

with great devotion and enthusiasm.

India has the largest Muslim population in the world after the Middle East. The Muslims in India follow their religion very scrupulously. They are in many ways still quite conservative and Muslim women in secular India still wear a "burqua", a garment that covers the entire body leaving only slits for the eyes. And even though the partition of the subcontinent has caused

in the west. That is not to say there are no tensions or separatist movements, but crises usually blow over and democracy prevails. It is no mere boast that India has not only the largest democracy in the world but one that is active and alive. Secularism, freedom and equality are not only enshrined in its constitution but practiced in everyday life. The majority follow Hinduism, which is more a philosophy and a way of life than a strict rules-laid-down religion. With a pantheon of Gods ranging from Brahma, the Creator, to Shiva, the Destroyer, Hindus have many festival days that are celebrated

Whether it is to celebrate a marriage or a festival, Hindus like to come out in procession so that there is a sense of community participation. With garlands round their necks and accompanied by musical instruments, a festive crowd congregates in Old Delhi.

a rift between the two communities, there is still much give and take, especially on festive occasions.

The Jains follow the teachings of Mahavira, the 24th "tirthankara" or saint. They believe in non-violence and are total vegetarians. More orthodox Jains still cover their noses and mouths with a mask to prevent their breathing in live germs and insects. They are a small but very rich, non-controversial community. The enormous statue of Bahubali at Sravanabelagola in Karnataka is an important place of Jain pilgrimage.

The Sikh religion arose from a fusion of the best ideas of Hinduism and Islam. As such, although it is a young religion, it is simple but vibrant. The tall, handsome bearded Sikhs you see wear the five 'Ks' the *Granth Sahib,* or the holy scriptures, demand of them — the *kirpan*, the *kada*, *kachha*, *kangi* and *kesh* — sword, bangle, underwear, comb, and hair.

India has a large Christian community of all denominations. St Thomas the Apostle was said to have landed in Cochin in 52 AD, from where Christianity has spread to the rest of the country. And the Catholics in India boast no less a person than Nobel laureate Mother Teresa.

even toilet and drinking-water facilities.

One of the things that hits one instantly in India is the poverty all around. This is such a great culture shock that often people only remember the beggars and the slums, the swollen-bellied, malnourished children and the starving dogs, cats and cows and forget everything else. That is because they don't see beyond the outward manifestations. The poorest of poor Indians is hospi-

The Parsees are the smallest of all religious communities but have probably contributed more to the industrial and scientific development of India than anyone else, with JRD Tata and Dr Homi Bhaba leading the list. Worshiping at fire temples, they neither cremate nor bury the dead but practice the unique custom of leaving the deceased in a "well of death" to be consumed by birds of prey.

A living, throbbing tradition, the contrasts and inconsistencies in this country are mind-boggling. Skyscrapers that would well compare with those in Tokyo or New York dot the azure blue skyline of Bombay, the pulsating business center and thriving metropolis on the west coast of India. Sprawled below, like festering sores, are the slums, many of which do not have

table to a sinful degree. Visit a village home or a slum house and if they have three spoonfuls of sugar they are saving up for the week they will spontaneously offer you two! Poverty hasn't made them selfish or greedy. They still have their dreams, their traditions, their culture. And if one can see *that*, the specter of poverty seems less grim.

Rents are exorbitant, be they apartments in skyscrapers or a hovel in a slum owned by a slum lord. This does not however prevent them from nurturing dreams of living comfortably and happily.

Rags to riches stories are a dime a dozen.

Twice a year an urs *fair is held to commemorate the anniversaries of the deaths of Nizam-ud-din Aulia, a 14th-century Muslim saint, and his disciple Amir Khusro. Hindu-Muslim unity is fostered on this occasion as friends of different religions greet each other.*

Initiative, talent and hard work do earn dividends. Dhirubhai Ambani, India's leading industrialist with a business empire that has an annual turnover of Rs 1,000 million (US $ 77 million) began life humbly as a clerk, then turned to trading before rising to his present status as a giant magnate.

Bullock carts, hand carts, horse-drawn *tongas* (carriages) and an unending stream of cycles and cycle rickshaws vie for space on the narrow roads of old Delhi with imported Mercedes, Toyotas, Suzukis as well as the sturdier Indian Ambassadors and Fiats and the popular lightweight Maruti. For thousands of people, cycles are still the primary means of transport.

Oxford and Harvard educated intellectuals with distinct foreign accents, and maharajas of yesteryears stripped of their titles and grandeur, rub shoulders with the hoi polloi. In contrast there are 400 million illiterate men, women and children. And there are over a 100 million tribals, many of them still living in the interiors of Bihar, Madhya Pradesh, Orissa and the Andaman and Nicobar Islands. Many of them still practice shifting cultivation, and some even today, have had no contact with modern civilization.

The Indian subcontinent is bound in the north by the snow-capped Himalayas. Everest, the world's highest peak, tall and beautiful, stands sentinel to the mountain range, as yet unspoilt by man's frequent incursions into its bosom. To its northwest lies Pakistan and the famous Hindu Kush mountains through which the Turks as well as the Mongols thundered into the plains of north India. To its north, and northwest lie Nepal, Tibet and China.

With a slight stretch of the imagination you can almost say India is heart-shaped. The warm waters of the Arabian Sea and the Bay of Bengal lap its western and eastern shores and tropical waves wash its southern tip.

India boasts of one of the world's earliest civilizations — the Indus Valley civilization was found in the Indian subcontinent in

At the beautiful Samodh Palace near Jaipur, a red carpet is rolled out to receive the erstwhile prince after his wedding. Now converted into a palace hotel, Samodh offers guests a glimpse of the glory of a vanished past.

Punjab and Sind and dates back to 2300 BC. With the partition of India in 1947, Mohenjodaro and Harappa, two city sites of the ancient civilization, went to Pakistan. But India has the Harappan sites at Ropar in Punjab and Lothal in Gujarat.

Recorded history begins with Alexander the Great's expedition in 327 BC and continues with a succession of dynasties or empires that laid the foundations of the India

turies before the birth of modern India's founding father, Mahatma Gandhi, Emperor Ashoka preached as well as practiced *ahimsa* or non-violence. It was during his reign that Buddhism flourished and spread to Southeast Asia. Though Ashoka was a devout Buddhist, stone inscriptions found all over the country bear testimony to his secular religious vision. One of the stone inscription says, "If you want to know your

of today. It is said that Alexander left his governers to rule his Indian conquests. Copper coins of the period bear testimony to the Greek influence in northwest India.

The vacuum created by the departure of Alexander was filled by Chandragupta Maurya who amalgamated the smaller states and formed the Mauryan empire.

The greatest of the Mauryas was undoubtedly Ashoka who after a bloody battle at Kalinga in Orissa was so overcome by remorse at the needless slaughter that he renounced his former way of life and became a zealous devotee of Buddha. Cen-

own religion better, sit at the feet of the preachers of other religions and you will find that all religions have something in common". Spiritually as well as materially it was an exciting time. Hinduism thrived along with Jainism and Buddhism and contact was established with Afghanistan, Syria, Iran and Egypt.

The golden era for India culture was under the Guptas in the fourth century. There was a rapid expansion in the education system with the opening of more schools and colleges.Philosophy and astronomy achieved new eminence. It was in the hey day of the Guptas that the famous Nalanda University was established in Bihar. At this time too, the poet-saint, Kalidasa set the note for future compositions in poetry. The rock temples and mural paintings of Ajanta and

Although princely India is no more, glimpses of past glory can still be seen, as in this picture of the former maharaja of Varanasi as he rides out in his royal carriage on the occasion of his birthday (above) and in a portrait shot with his grandson (right).

Historical Chronology

2300 – 1750 BC — The Indus Valley civilization or the "Harappan Culture" in Punjab, Sind, and areas of Rajasthan and Kathiawar, discovered in the 1920s, suggests a highly "urbanized" civilization noted for its town-planning.

1500 BC — The arrival of the Indo-Aryans, descendants of the Indo-Europeans in the northwest. A pastoral, cattle-breeding people they settle in the Punjab, Gangetic valley and as far south as the Vindhyas. Earliest of the *Rig Veda*, a collection of songs of prayers, hymns and ritual prescriptions, originates from this period.

600 BC — This period sees the rise of monarchies and republics in northern India. Various religious sects also arise with Buddhism and Jainism acquiring the status of major religions.

327 BC — Alexander of Macedon campaigns in northwestern India. His premature death prevents the consolidation of his Indian exploits.

321 BC — The Mauryan empire, the first form of "imperial" government in India, takes root. Chandragupta Maurya establishes power and hegemony in central and northwest India.

273 BC — Ashoka, one of the greatest monarchs ascends the throne. After his successful conquest of Kalinga, he denounces war and embraces Buddhism. A variety of sources suggest a centralized, highly efficient administration and bureaucracy and flourishing trade and crafts.

200 BC – **200** AD — A series of Indo-Greek invasions takes place. Indo-Greek King Menander conquers areas in Punjab and Mathura near Delhi. An intermingling of Greek and Indian cultures leads to the famous Gandhara school of sculpture.

180 BC — Mauryan power declines. Its disintegration gives rise to a number of small kingdoms such as the Sunga dynasty in Magadh and Central India and Kalinga under its ruler Kharavela.

57 BC — Entry of the Shakas, a foreign tribe from Central Asia, on the Indian scene.

87 – 144 AD — The Kushan dynasty begins its reign — one of the significant phases in the cultural development of northern India. The Mathura school of art flourishes. Kanishka, one of its greatest kings rules over his kingdom from Purushapura.

106 – 130 — Ascent of the Satavahana power in the Deccan — the successors of the Mauryans in that region. Rock-cut caves and Buddhist stupas belong to this period.

320 — Chandragupta I founds the Gupta dynasty which is often referred to as the "Classical Age" or the "Golden Age" of India. During his reign Hindu culture is firmly established in northern India. His successor, Samudragupta, consolidates the Gupta power and hegemony and pushes it further south.

375 – 415 — Samudragupta's son, Chandragupta II, also known as Vikramaditya defeats the Shakas in western India. Fa Hsien, the Chinese Buddhist pilgrim, visits India during this period and paints a glowing and comprehensive account of the country. Under the Guptas arts and literature flourish and scholars and poets like Kalidasa and Amarasimha are patronized. Ajanta paintings, the greatest of Buddhist art, also come from this period.

600 – 630 — In the south, several important kingdoms emerge — with the Pallavas and the Chalukyas being the most prominent. This is followed by a period of conflict in which the Pallavas under Narasimhavarman defeat the Cholas, Cheras and Pandyas. The famous rock-cut temples at Mahabalipuram belong to this period.

606 – 647 — Rise of Harshavardhana or "Harsha" of the Pushyabhuti family. Making Kanauj the seat of his power he extends his authority in all directions. A detailed account of this period survives in the writing of court poet Banabhatta's *Harshacharitra*.

900 — Anangpal, a Rajput ruler, builds Lal Kot, said to be the first city of Delhi.

907 — Parantaka I, the Chola ruler, establishes Chola power in the south. Rajendra I succeeds and continues the policy of expansion. The Chola period is known for its architecture and for its bronze sculptures and figurines.

1000 — Sultan Mahmud of Ghazni begins his raids from the northern frontier. He attacks seventy times in a period of seventeen years and paves the way for the rule of the Turks and Afghans in India. Muhammed Ghori also conducts vigorous campaigns of expansion into northern

India towards the end of the 12th century.

1206 — Muhammed Ghori is murdered and his general Qutb-ud-Din Aibak assumes control of his Indian possessions. This lays the foundation of what is known as the "Delhi Sultanate".

1211 – 86 — Aibak's son-in-law Iltumish rules. To him goes the credit of firmly establishing the Turkish rule in India. He completes the famous monument Qutb Minar.

1266 — Balban ascends the throne and consolidates the power of the Delhi sultanate.

1296 – 1316 — Ala-ud-Din Khalji rules. His reign marks the highest point of the Sultanate's political power in terms of extent of empire and authority of the sultan. He lays the foundation of the second city of Delhi, Siri.

1320 — Ghiyas-ud-Din Tughluq wrests power and establishes a new dynasty, the Tughluqs. The third city of Delhi, Tughlaqabad, is raised by him.

1325 – 51 — Muhammed Bin Tughluq reigns. An innovative ruler he is regarded by historians as a visionary whose fantastic ideas were out of tune with the times. He builds Jahanpanah, the fourth city, between Lal Kot and Siri.

1351 — Firuz Shah Tughluq, known for his benevolent measures, succeeds to the throne. He builds Firuzabad, the fifth city, on the western banks of the Yamuna. After him, the power and influence of the sultanate starts to decline.

1398 — Timur, the dreaded Turk, attacks India and strikes the last blow to the Tughluq dynasty. The Tughluqs are succeeded by the Sayyids who only just manages to keep the sultanate going.

1451 – 1596 — The Lodis of Afghan descent rule. This period sees inter-tribal rivalries which finally leads to the eclipse of the dynasty.

1526 — Babur, a descendent of Timur, invades India. He lays the foundation of the Mughul rule in India.

1540 — Babur dies and he is succeeded by his son Humayun who establishes the foundation of the sixth city, Din Panah, at the site of the Purana Qila.

1556 — Akbar becomes the emperor and the Mughal dynasty soars to new heights. The greatest of the Mughal kings, he abolishes Jizya, a religious tax and marries a Rajput princess, Jodha Bai, the sister of Raja Man Singh in an effort to bring different religious groups together. Twenty-six years after assuming power he begins construction of his famous capital, Fatehpur Sikri, and promulgates his religion, Din Ilahxi.

1600 — The London East India is granted charter.

Other colonial powers too make their inroads into the Indian subcontinent. In 1605, the United East India Company of the Netherlands is formed and four years later the Dutch company is established at Pulicat in Tamil Nadu. In 1613, Jehangir grants *firman* (permission) to the East India Company and they begin trade with Bengal soon after.

1630 — Shivaji, the greatest of the Maratha rulers, who would later harass both the British and declining Mughal empire, is born in Maharashtra.

1638 — Shah Jahan, the fifth Mughal ruler, lays the foundation for Shahjahanabad, the seventh city, with the Red Fort at Delhi as its citadel.

1666 — The greatest of the Mughal architects, Shah Jahan, who constructed the beautiful Taj Mahal at Agra and the Red Fort at Delhi dies. In 1707, with the death of his son, Aurangzeb, the Mughal empire begins to disintegrate.

1739 — Nadir Shah, a Persian ruler, invades Delhi and carts off the Peacock Throne amidst much violence and killing.

1744 — Frenchman, Joseph Francois Dupleix, is appointed governor of Pondicherry in the south. In east India the English capture Chandernagore. With the battle of Arcot near Madras in 1751 the domination of the French is broken. In 1765, Robert Clive is appointed governor of Bengal.

1769/70 — The great Bengal famine occurs. The estimates of dead vary from three to ten million.

1793 — British rule in India gains ascendancy! The permanent settlement of land revenue, whereby a fixed amount is taken as tax from the peasants, is signed between the rulers of Bengal and the British. In 1801, Karnataka becomes a part of British empire.

1853 — First railway in India from Bombay to Thane is introduced, and for the first time Indians are allowed to sit for the Indian civil service in open competition with the British.

1857 — Sepoy mutiny at Meerut breaks out. It is the first expression of revolt by the suppressed Indians which spreads all over north India

1876 — Queen Victoria is proclaimed Empress of India.

1885 — The Indian National Congress is formed. A British civil servant, Mr AD Hune, founds the party, but Mr WC Bonnerji, a Calcutta barister, is appointed its first president. Several prominent Indians like Dadabhai Naoroji attend the Bombay meeting.

1905 — The British partition Bengal in an effort to break the national movement but are unsuccessful and cannot cope with the patriotic upsurge. Khudiram Bose, 18, gives vent to the growing anti-British feelings by throwing a bomb which kills two British ladies in Bengal in 1908. He is sentenced to death.

1911 — King George the V holds coronation durbar at Delhi and proclaims the shifting of the capital from Calcutta to Delhi.

1930 — The anti-British campaign gathers momentum in India. A salt march is held in Dandi, Gujarat, to break salt laws and many people are arrested. Gandhiji begins the civil disobedience movement and is arrested. A round table conference is held in England to discuss India's independence.

1940 — Mr MA Jinnah in a presidential address at the Lahore session of the All-India Muslim League demands separate homeland for Muslims and passes a resolution for creation of Pakistan.

1942 — Quit India Resolution is passed by the Congress Working Committee. In Bangkok, Subhash Chandra Bose forms the Indian National Army and General Mohan Singh is appointed its commander-in-chief.

1945 — Interim government is formed in India but Jinnah reiterates his demand for a separate Muslim state and refuses to join the interim government.

1947 — Partition of India results in a bloodbath. The Indian domination is established at midnight August 15 and Jawaharlal Nehru is appointed first Prime Minister.

1948 — The father of the Nation, Gandhiji, is shot dead at a prayer meeting at Tees January Marg by Nathu Ram Godse. The nation is plunged into gloom. Lord Louis Mountbatten, India's first governor-general, leaves for England and Dr C Rajagopalachari is appointed in his place.

1950 — India is proclaimed a sovereign democractic republic on January 26. Dr Rajendra Prasad becomes President of the Indian Republic.

1962 — In October, China launches a massive attack on India in the north-eastern and Ladakh areas. On November 21 a ceasefire is announced. India suffers a humiliating defeat and she decides to strengthen its armed forces.

1964 — Jawaharlal Nehru, India's first Prime Minister dies. Mr Lal Bahadur Shastri is elected leader of the Congress Party and sworn in as the second Prime Minister of the country.

1965 — Indo-Pak conflict results when Pakistan invades Indian territory. The Soviet Union invites leaders from both sides for talks to resolve differences. Within hours of signing the agreement with the Pakistani President at Tashkent in 1966, Mr

Shastri dies on Soviet soil on January 24. Mrs Indira Gandhi is sworn in as Prime Minister.

1971 — Second Indo-Pak conflict in December culminates in the surrender of Pakistani troops to the Indian Army in Dacca. Bangladesh is born and an agreement is signed with India for unified military command.

1975 — After the Allahabad High Court set aside Mrs Indira Gandhi's elections on charges of corruption in electioneering practices, a state of emergency is declared and opposition leaders and dissident congressmen are arrested. Later, the Supreme Court upholds Mrs Gandhi's election.

1977 — In March, elections are held and the Congress Party is routed. The opposition parties who unite under the banner of the Janata party form the first non-Congress government with Mrs Morarji Desai as Prime Minister. A rift in the Janata Party in 1979 causes Morarji Desai to step down and Mr Charan Singh becomes leader of the coalition government.

1980 — Elections are held and Mrs Indira Gandhi and those who stayed loyal to her come back with a thumping majority. Sanjay Gandhi, Mrs Indira Gandhi's younger son, is appointed secretary of the Congress but he dies in an airplane crash soon after, in June.

1984 — The demand for a separate Sikh state, Khalistan, is countered by the Indian Army launching a frontal attack and entering the Golden Temple at Amritsar on June 3. Among those killed is Jarnail Singh Bhindranwale, a *granthi* (religious leader) who spearheaded the movement for Khalistan. The religious Sikhs are offended and swear revenge. On October 31 Mrs Indira Gandhi is assassinated by her Sikh bodyguard in the garden of her house. Mr Rajiv Gandhi, Mrs Gandhi's older son assumes the post of Prime Minister. Hindu/Sikh riots break out and hundreds of Sikhs are slaughtered.

1984 Dec — Elections are held and Mr Rajiv Gandhi sweeps the polls winning by a three-fourths majority. Out of 495 seats in the Lok Sabha, the Congress claims 401.

1984 Dec 3 — Union Carbide tragedy occurs in Bhopal. Escaping gas from tanks in the plant takes a heavy toll of lives.

1987 — India and Sri Lanka sign a peace accord to end the communal conflict between the Central Government and the Tamil separatist fighters in Sri Lanka.

1989 Nov — Elections are held and the Congress Party fails to gain majority. A coalition government is formed with V P Singh as Prime Minister.

Ellora testify to the glory of that era.

Five hundred years later the Chola dynasty of the south dominated the Indian canvas leaving its distinctive mark on buildings and architecture. Chola bronzes were exquisite pieces of workmanship and in demand the world over today. The superb dancing Nataraja effigies in bronze are creations of that period.

In the 13th century the Turks came to

and Shalimar gardens of Kashmir. Miniature paintings on ivory and cloth flourished and Kathak, a graceful dance of swirls and foot beats within rhythmic patterns acquired the status of a court dance.

Akbar, the great Mughal emperor whose first wife was a Hindu, Jodha Bai, laid the foundations of a secularism still practiced to this day. His grandson, Shah Jahan, immortalized his love for his wife, Mumtaz,

India and stayed for 200 years leaving for posterity the Qutb Minar, the 72.5 meters high victory tower cum minaret in South Delhi. Though the foundations of this exquisite minaret were laid by Qutb-ud-din Aibak, subsequent rulers added to it as well as repaired it.

Then came the Mughals who left an indelible mark on India's art, architecture and culture. Some of the finest monuments of the world — the Taj Mahal and Fatehpur Sikri at Agra, and the Red Fort and Jama Masjid in Delhi — were built by them. Their love for gardens nurtured the Nishat Bagh

*India's mountain ranges, particularly the Himalayas (**above**), intrigues and inspires mountaineers, photographers and nature lovers. In the monsoons, clouds play hide-and-seek in the Himalayan peaks which come winter will soon be draped in a mantle of white.*

in the most perfect monument in marble — the Taj Mahal.

The coming of the Muslims to India added richness and variety to social life and manners. They were great patrons of art, music, poetry and language.

From the late fourteenth century itself covetous eyes were cast on India's gold — encrusted temples, gem-studded idols, its spices, fabulous silks and fine cotton textiles. In 1498 Vasco da Gama landed at Calicut in South India. Twelve years later Goa fell to the Portugese who left India only in 1960.

The French, Dutch and British came to India in the 17th century to establish trade links, but stayed on to conquer and rule. The British domination was complete. They turned India into their biggest colony and reigned supreme till a non-violent movement inspired by a dhoti-clad figure, Mahatma Gandhi, forced them to leave the Indian shores in 1947.

The nearly two hundred years of British rule in India influenced not just the education, culture and thinking of the local people but was reflected in art and architecture. They created New Delhi, one of the finest capitals of the world, with broad, open boulevards, tree lined avenues and exquisite gardens. The British architect, Edwin Lutyens, visualized, landscaped and constructed the central complex of New Delhi and built Rashtrapati Bhavan, the President's house on Raisina Hill, overlooking one of the most beautiful avenues in the world. Long, rectangular pools of water on either side of the road soothe the eyes and the spirit.

Two kilometers across from the President's house stands India Gate, the memorial to the soldiers who laid down their lives in the world war.

The westernization of India began with the British. Though it is 40 years since they have left the subcontinent, the English language continues to be the link language and has been recognized as the national language along with Hindi. There have been several attempts to replace English with Hindi and other regional languages but by and large these have failed. In states like Nagaland in the east, English is the state language. The departing British partitioned India and created the Muslim-dominated Pakistan in the northwest and east Pakistan (now Bangladesh), leading to communal riots and a bloodbath that has left permanent scars on both countries.

Despite the growing number of educated non-believers, India is a deeply religious country. Every village and city in this country is dotted with temples, mosques, Sikh gurdwaras and churches. Sometimes a temple, mosque and church can be found in the same complex. The Parsee fire temples can be seen primarily in Bombay. Some cities, particularly in the south, even have Jewish synagogues.

The abode of the Gods — whether it is Birla Mandir in Delhi, Meenakshi Temple in Madurai, Tirupati Temple on the outskirts of Madras, Jama Masjid in Delhi or the cathedrals of Goa or the Golden Temple at Amritsar — are grand structures visited not only as places of pilgrimage but as tourist attractions. The religious rich bestow largesse at these places of

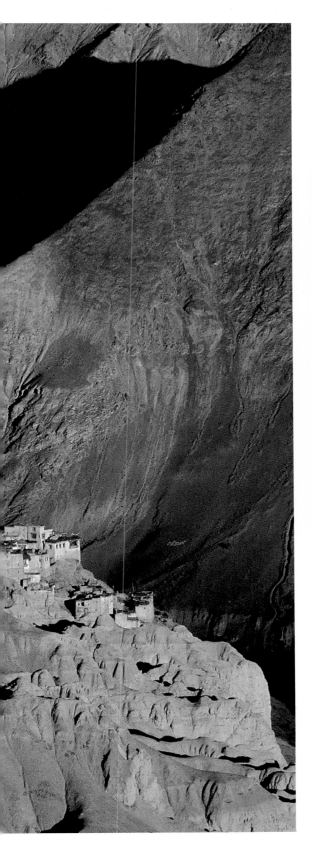

worship for vows fulfilled and to ensure themselves salvation.

The coffers of many of the famous temples and gurdwaras are overflowing with gold as well as hard currency offered by devotees. The richest temple in the country is the Venkateshwara Temple in Tirupati where the deity is said to be extraordinarily powerful. Barbers do a brisk business here because Venkateshwara's favorite offering

is hair and men and women with newly-tonsured billiard ball heads walk about unselfconsciously.

The domes of the Akal Takht and Harminder Sahib in the Golden Temple at Amritsar are covered with fine beaten gold that glistens like halos in the fierce summer sun. At night they glow mellow in the moonlight. The foreign tourists used as they are to guarding their traveler's checks and foreign exchange are surprised that no one touches the temple gold.

Fairs and festivals are the most colorful manifestations of religion. Rich and poor

*Tucked high up in the mountains of Ladakh, snow-bound four to five months of the year, is this bleak but picturesque ancient monastery of Lamayuru (**left**), while (**above**) hidden behind a screen of bare poplars is a typical village hut of rural Ladakh.*

alike wear their best clothes and jewelry and join in the fun once the rituals are over. In India, people use any excuse for celebration. Festivals celebrate the seasons, a good harvest, births, weddings and exploits of legendary heroes. The arrival of a new moon is celebrated as is its maturation to fullness. Cattle fairs where everything from camels, and elephants to horses, bullocks and sheep are sold, begin with sports, frolic and some

For nine days work comes to a virtual standstill during the Durga puja celebrations in West Bengal and Orissa. Durga symbolises "shakti" or primordial energy and is worshiped as the destroyer of evil. For weeks before the celebrations begin, there is a frenzy of activity. In Kumartuli, Calcutta's potters lane, clay effigies of Durga start taking shape. Till the moment before the statues are installed with pomp and

religious ceremony.

Of all the festivals in India the gayest is Diwali, the festival of light, celebrated when the moon is in the dark phase in September or October. After *puja* or prayers in the evening, traditional earthern lamps are lit to invite the Goddess of Wealth, Lakshmi, to step in and bless the house. After that, fireworks shatter the velvet dark night in a kaleidoscope of color.

Colors literally fly at Holi, the festival that heralds the hot summer months. It is a boisterous community festival where friends, relations and even strangers chuck myriad-hued powdered colors at one another or even hurl bucketfuls of colored water! Unfortunately, the festival often degenerates into hooliganism brought on quite often by the imbibing of intoxicant *bhang*.

ceremony last minute decorations lend the finishing touches. Shops, particularly cloth shops, do brisk business as it is customary to give clothes as gifts. As the festival draws to a close on the tenth day — Vijaya Dasami — the excitement reaches a feverish pitch and only dies down with the immersion of the images in the holy Ganges.

One of the loveliest festivals is Raksha Bandhan which sanctifies the bond between brother and sister. A colorful *rakhi* is tied on the brother's wrist by the sister as a protection against all evils and hazards.

The golden sand dunes of Rajasthan come

A baby receives his early morning ablutions oblivious to his surroundings (left). All over Bombay you can see the coexistence of slums and skyscrapers, of poverty and wealth. A vendor (above) hitches an early morning ride on the back of a crowded Calcutta bus.

alive for the Pushkar Mela, the biggest cattle fair of the state held in the month of November. Camel races, beauty contests to select the handsomest of the desert ship, a bazaar that sells everything from harnesses and saddles for camels and horses to glass and ivory bangles for womenfolk are just some of the attractions of this popular fair. There is a brisk sale of animals, plenty of fun and games and before the villagers return home they have a dip in the holy waters of Pushkar Lake and cleanse themselves of all their sins.

For centuries, sadhus and godmen have been an integral part of India's spiritual life. But at no time is their impressive presence felt as at Kumbh Mela, a fair held once every 12 years. The fair is held at four places — Hardwar, Allahabad, Ujjain and Nasik.

Of these the most important is the one at Allahabad, said to be the confluence of three rivers — Ganges, Yamuna and the invisible Saraswati.

The grand spectacle of hundreds of naked sadhus coming in procession to the ghats with their tridents and *kamandalams* (bowl-shaped iron vessels), some on gaily decorated elephants and horses, automatically gets them the right of way. Jostling, stampeding crowds respectfully stand by as the godmen with their matted tresses and ash-covered bodies make their way to the river. An enduring image of the mela is the "deep-

Bombay is India's second most populous city. Space on the island is limited and even matinee idols and business tycoons have to live in multi-storied buildings (above). At Nariman Point, the Oberoi Hotel (right) takes pride of place in the changing cityscape.

While the snake is venerated in India, for many it also provides a means of livelihood. Here, in front of the Red Fort (**below**), a snake handler gets his pet python ready to entertain a tourist crowd.

Of Snakes and Snake Worship

To most westerners, India conjures up visions of tigers, snakes and snake charmers. No wonder in most cities outside big hotels you can see the snake charmer playing the "been" while snakes sway in a hypnotic trance.

India with its lush forests and tropical climate abounds in over 200 species of snakes. Of these, only four are poisonous — the king cobra, other cobra species, the viper and the krait.

Till the ban on export of snake skins, snakes were being caught in millions and skinned for export. For some, like the Irulas of Tamil Nadu, it was their sole means of livelihood. It is part of the dichotomy that is India that while some people exploit the snake commercially others continue to revere and worship it. The naga (snake) has held a hallowed place in Indian mythology — the cobra forming a garland around the neck of Lord Shiva and the anantnag, the many-hooded serpent, providing shade for Lord Vishnu and even forming a couch on which he reclined.

Throughout the country the snake god is worshiped and the fifth day of shravan (the Indian calendar) in July or August is celebrated as Nagapanchmi — the day of the snake. Unboiled milk is offered to the snake god on that day. In some places, images of the snake god are drawn on walls for worship and in others cloth, metal and stone images are worshiped.

But worship of a live snake is considered the most auspicious. In Srirala, a small village near Sangli, Maharashtra, thousands of snakes are actually caught for worship. The trapping begins a month before Nagapanchmi with the villagers digging them out of their burrows and pits. A forked stick is used to pin down their head and with the other hand they catch the snake. The snakes are then placed in an earthern pot which is kept covered and strung on trees. Throughout the month the trapping continues but the fangs and venom are never removed.

On the day of worship hundreds of pots are taken out on a bullock cart and village youths dance along wearing snakes around their necks like garlands. The snake pots are taken to a temple for worship. After worship they are returned to the villagers who take them out of their pots for display. An earthern pot containing pebbles is rolled in front of the snakes to hold their attention as they emerge from the pots. This is followed by competitions to test the skill of snake handlers.

Sometimes a handler or an innocent bystander is bitten and dies but these occasional accidents have not diminished the fervor of the festival. On the contrary, no work is done on Nagapanchmi in the fields or at home for fear of unwittingly harming the snake.

Towards evening the snakes are released and rushed back to their subterranean refuge till the next Nagapanchmi.

No festival or auspicious occasion begins without an invocation to the lovable elephant god, Ganesha **(below).** Bombay is the place to witness the Ganesh festival where idols are worshiped and taken out in grand processions to be immersed in the sea.

The God with the Mostest

Every July and August, towards the end of the monsoons, the streets of the Western Ghats of Maharashtra resound with this enthusiastic chant as enormous idols are taken in mind-boggling processions for immersion in the Arabian Sea.

> Ganapathi Bapa morya
> Pudcha varsha lavkarya
>
> "Beloved Ganapathi, return
> quickly to us next year".

This is the climax of the 10-day festival dedicated to Ganapathi. Ganapati (or Ganesha or Vinayaka) is the god with the "mostest"! Ask anyone in India who their favorite god is and without exception they will all say "Ganesha"! No wonder Ganesha the elephant-headed god is worshiped at all times. No auspicious event takes place unless Ganesha is propitiated. No undertaking, whether it be the starting of a long journey, the construction of a house, any examination and certainly all religious festivals, takes place without first offering prayers to Ganesha. Endearingly rotund, Ganesha is the remover of all obstacles.

And he has many other amiable attributes too. Like the elephant whose head he wears, he has an infallible memory. He is great in spiritual and worldly affairs. He is the god of wisdom and learning and is himself very learned. Sage Vyasa who conceived the great Indian epic, the Mahabharata, dictated it to Ganesha. Ganesha who had agreed to write it down, laid down only two conditions. One, that the dictation should flow smoothly and two, that at all times he must be able to understand and clearly follow what was being said. That is why it is said that the Mahabharata is one of the most mellifluous of epics.

There are many versions about how Ganesha came by his elephant's head. One, the most popular of all was like this. Shiva (the Destroyer) liked to surprise his consort Parvati by appearing when she was having a bath but Parvati did not appreciate it at all. So one day, she took the surf from her body, mixed it with other elements, shaped it to look like a man and sprinkled Ganga water on it which immediately brought the figure to life. She asked him to stand guard while she was in her bath and to let no one enter. But of course, Shiva turned up and when he was barred entrance, in a great rage he cut off Ganesha's head. Parvati was so distraught with grief that Shiva sent out messengers to look for a substitute head. The first living creature they saw was an elephant. They cut off its head and brought it to Shiva who fixed it to the trunk and Parvati was appeased!

Although Ganesha is the major deity in Maharashtra, he is only found in the sitting or standing posture. In the south, you can also come across a dancing Ganesha. One of the famous Ganesha temples is the Ashtavinayaka (eight Vinayaks), temple near Pune. The Ganesha there is said to grant all desires.

Food is a high priority with Vinayaka as his enormous potbelly bears out. Of all food, his greatest favorite is modak, a sweet made with rice and stuffed with jaggery and coconut. But he doesn't turn up his trunk at any other kind of food either!

A quaint custom is associated with Ganesha. In the face of insurmountable difficulties or excessive hardships, a Ganesha idol is immersed in water and left like that. The idea is that only a God put into difficulty can understand the distress that someone else is going through. Often, as the water evaporates, the troubled period also blows over!

patras" (tiny boats made from heart-shaped peepul leaves) floating on the waters with lighted oil flames. As they travel down the river at dusk, it seems as if the river has come alive with a million fireflies.

The first thing that hits one in India is the millions and millions of people all of whom seem to be trying to make their presence felt. They surge on the roads, the beaches and the crowded public transport system. Whether it is Bombay's highly efficient suburban trains, the notorious public buses of the Delhi Transport Corporation or the leisurely trams of Calcutta, it is not easy to get a toe-hold in the rush hour. In Delhi, the buses almost keel over with the weight of passengers hanging on to the side and back of the buses. In Srinagar, a bus ride into the countryside can be a bizarre experience with hens, chicken and other table birds traveling to the market along with the regular commuters. While some birds are trussed up in baskets, others are carried by the scruff of their neck or by just hanging on to their clawing legs. Suddenly a bird gets loose and there is loud squawking and cursing as the bird lands on the head or lap of a passenger.

Getting off a bus or a suburban train is as much of a problem as getting in. You may be hurtled out of the bus by the crowds behind you or you may just miss your stop. The moral of the story is that a journey on the public transport system is always adventurous. It is also the only means of transport for India's masses.

India's railway literally groan and creak with the enormous responsibility of carrying millions of people and freight from one end of the country to another. It takes almost three days to reach India's southernmost tip from Delhi. Bombay and Calcutta are almost 24 hours away from the capital, though there are a few fast trains that reduce the journey by six to eight hours. Trains and railway stations are almost as crowded as the buses in the big cities. It is virtually impossible to travel by rail without reservations made in advance.

Traveling by train can be a memorable experience if you are easy, accommodating, do not mind the human crush or the Indian's curiosity and loquacity. Indians have

The video boom has not sullied the charm of the cinema. Huge cinema hoardings are constantly going up in Delhi to announce a new film and the latest star on the horizon. The Indian film industry is among the world's largest in terms of output of films.

no airs about them and do not stand on ceremony. They open their hearts and homes to comparative strangers as they share the endless food boxes they carry on long journeys.

Not all trains have restaurant cars but at every railway station you are besieged by petty traders selling fruits, bangles and *chai* (tea) in small disposal earthern containers. In the south, coffee is served by the yard as

green with little mountain streams zigzagging through them.

The most comfortable means of traveling the subcontinent by rail is by air-conditioned first-class. Second class travel may give you the flavor of India but it is distinctly uncomfortable — hot, dusty, steamy and a "crushing" experience!

H eat and dust are intrinsic to India. Eight to nine months of the year it is

vendors skilfully stretch the brew between a small steel vessel and a glass! It's a sight not to be missed and the froth on the coffee is as good as any whipped up by a modern espresso machine.

Though a major section of the railways is electrified there are still 8,000 steam locomotives huffing and puffing down hills and valleys adding to the quaint charm of India. Large tracts of the country are still connected by meter gauge and the bogies are small and narrow.

There is a similarity between the Swiss trains and the hill trains of India built by the British to enable foreigners to escape the summer heat of the plains. They are delightful little trains winding their way at a leisurely pace through the most picturesque hills of India, many of them still emerald

hot and uncomfortable in most parts of the country except in the north and northeast of India and at the hill stations. In May and June the mercury fluctuates between 42 degrees celsius and 50 degrees celsius and in the deserts it could rise even higher. It is virtually impossible to work or wander around after midday and a siesta would seem the most rational thing to do.

Delhi, barely 200 kilometers from the Rajasthan deserts, burns and wilts as the mercury soars at midday. In the height of summer its roads are almost desolate and white heat rises in waves from the metalled

Calcutta is one of the most populated cities of the world where thousands of people sleep and live on the pavements. The film posters on the city walls like the one above often serve as colorful but macabre decorations for their roofless abodes.

*Regional characteristics and costumes prevail despite modernization. India's color-ful ethnic mosaic includes (**top left to right**) a turbaned young Nihang Sikh, a sadhu, a Punjabi lady, a Rajasthani village girl and (**bottom left to right**) a Kashmiri man and woman, a Ladakhi woman and an Arunachal Pradesh tribal belle.*

roads. Beneath shade-giving trees at road junctions are placed huge earthern pitchers with cool water from which the thirsty quench their thirst. Gallons of water have to be guzzled in the summer months to keep down the heat and cold drink and ice-cream vendors do a roaring business.

One of the most beautiful sights is the breaking of the monsoons. After months of intense, scorching heat, the skies fill with low, heavy black clouds that thunder ominously. Lightning illuminates the darkness at noon. Suddenly like floodgates opened the rains pour down on the parched earth. The earth-laden smell of the first monsoon rains is unforgettable. Naked children rush out to the roads and parks dancing in the rain. There is great rejoicing through the land. Although India is progressive and is poised for a take-off into the 20th century, one of its inexplicable paradoxes is that it is completely dependent on its monsoons for irrigation. If it does not rain, specters of drought loom on the horizon. If the monsoon is on schedule and it rains enough, the granaries fill up, there are no power cuts and industry prospers.

The monsoons have their own romance. In Bombay the rough sea waves lash the embankments of Marine Drive and fall across the road in giant cascades. Nature lovers, the young and uninhibited and the romantic roll up their trousers or hitch up their saris and go for long walks in the rain. It's fun to get wet and there is no use trying to carry an umbrella for there is every possibility of it getting blown away. Eating hot corn on the cob roasted on impromptu fires and spiced with a dash of salt and lime is one of the monsoon delights.

Poor drainage system quickly turns roads whether in Delhi, Bombay or Calcutta, into rivers or huge ponds in which the cars and buses pack up. For the little urchins who seem to suddenly descend on this water-logged scene from nowhere, pushing the marooned cars is almost as much fun as dancing in the rain. And it's also an opportunity to make some quick money.

But with uninterrupted torrential rains, rivers which were thin ribbons in summer get angry and swollen and rush down in devastating torrents often sweeping aside entire villages. Life in India is never placid or predictable.

If you want to get the real feel and flavor of India, walk through the weekly bazaar. Each locality in the city has its own little market which is similar to a flea market. Makeshift shops sprawl across the roads and crowds jostle and push to get the best bargain. Everything from vegetables, pickles, crockery, textiles, second-hand coats, trousers, sweaters to simple footwear can be bought at the bazaar at throwaway

prices. This is the shopping center of the middle classes who come to buy what may be just an ordinary looking mug or a sari. India is an amazing place for handmade goods. And one is not talking about beautiful handicrafts. Even everyday things can be made to order.

In winter, quilts are made before customers on the streets. Mountains of cotton of differing quality are piled up in one corner. At an adjoining shop, quilt covers of velvet, satin and cotton are on sale. The required quality of cotton is purchased and in no time a man is whipping it up to fluffiness

*The Madhubani painters of Bihar traditionally decorated the mud walls of their village huts. Today these painters put their talents to more commercial use such as this artist (**left and above**) who paints images of deities on art paper for a living.*

The Wonderful World of Wildlife

How can you come to India and not see its magnificent king of the jungles, the tiger? Or the herds of wild elephants, the barasingha (the 12-horned deer) and the Indian one-horned rhinoceros.

One of the greatest wildlife success stories is that of the Indian tiger. From a population of 40,000 at the turn of the century it had dropped to 1,827 in 1927 causing it to be among the endangered list of the International Union for Conservation of Nature. In the massive campaign launched to save the tiger not only this supreme predator but all its prey species got a new lease on life. Today there are over 4,000 tigers in the 16 reserves of the country.

Barely 200 to 300 kilometers from New Delhi are three tiger reserves — the Corbett National Park in Uttar Pradesh, and the Sariska and Ranthambhor wildlife sanctuaries in Rajasthan — where you can see the tiger in all its magnificence.

Corbett Park, named after the legendary Jim Corbett is also home to other animals big and small. Here tigers, leopards, panthers, elephants, crocodiles, sambars and over 580 species of birds all live together maintaining a harmonious balance.

At Corbett no one is allowed to venture into the forests without an armed escort for sudden encounters with a wild elephant, particularly a rogue, can be terrifying. The keen tourists to the park do not rest till they have spotted the elusive tiger. With heightened senses, pounding hearts, they traverse the jungles from sunrise to well after sunset for a glimpse of the splendid beast. You can come across one suddenly, ambling across the valley or lying in the bush by the roadside or, if you are really lucky, you may see a tigress playing with her cubs.

The best way to look for a tiger is to go into the marshy interiors and tall grass on elephants. The tamed elephants and their mahouts are only too eager to escort the tourists. As you keep swaying through the thick undergrowth on elephant back, the mahout regales you with innumerable stories about encounters with tigers.

Visitors to the Ranthambhor wildlife sanctuary never go back disappointed. Despite the limited size of the park and a population of about 35 to 40 tigers you may see a handful of tigers on the same day. The big cats have become so used to visitors that they can be seen staring with bored, yellowed flecked eyes at the packed jeeps. Of all tiger reserves it is easiest to spot a tiger in

India's wildlife sanctuaries and national parks harbor a wide variety of animal life and offer visitors a chance to see the animals in their protected natural environments. Many rare species such as the Indian one-horned rhino are making a come back.

the open grasslands of Ranthambhor.

Sariska, another wildlife sanctuary, is just four hours away from the capital by car. Besides the prospect of sighting a tiger, a visit to the park is always exciting for it is a rare synthesis of natural history and archeology. You can see the ruins of the 9th century Shiva temples of Garj, Rajer and the medieval fort of Kanokwari. The luster of the landscape in winter turns into a splendid mosaic of grey-red with the blooming of the flame of the forest from March to April.

The other fabulous tiger reserve is Kanha in Madhya Pradesh. You can fly to Jabalpur, then drive across to the solitude and splendor of Kanha. This is one of the best managed tiger parks with a population of over 90 tigers. Nestling in the Mekal chain of hills, it presents a breathtaking panorama of sparsely wooded grassy plateaus, sprawling slopes covered with trees, giant bamboo and endless vistas of sal trees.

But perhaps the most splendid tiger sanctuary of all is in the tropical mangrove forests of the Sunderbans. Still relatively untouched by development, the Sunderbans are a picture of wild natural beauty. And that is the true home of the Royal Bengal tiger that has adapted to the salt-water environment. It is the only tiger in the world that catches fish for food! This sprawling national park situated in the delta estuaries of the Ganga and the Brahmaputra has over 265 tigers.

While the tiger has many homes, the highly endangered great Indian rhino's principal home is in Kaziranga, Assam. By translocating some of the rhinos, a second home is coming up at Dudhwa National Park. Surrounded on all sides by tea estates the rhino is completely at home in the tall elephant grass and marshy lands of Kaziranga.

Another greatly endangered species is the majestic barasingha (12-horned deer) which can be seen only in the Kanha reserve. At the Kanha forest lodge you can sit out on the verandah and watch a herd of spotted barasingha foraging for food. During the rutting season the peace of the forest is disturbed by barasingha battling with their horns for the leadership of the herd.

Three hours from Delhi and barely an hour's drive from Agra is the Bharatpur Bird Sanctuary, the home of thousands of birds. Migratory Siberian cranes, ducks and teals stop at Bharatpur in their annual journey to warmer climes. Ornithologists and bird lovers from India and abroad come to this extraordinary piece of wetlands to study birds and to spend a few days of peace. For after all, who can resist the call of the wild.

with ancient hand-operated machine whose thwack and whirr add to the cacophony of sounds of an Indian bazaar. As the quilts are being filled and stitched there is time to browse around shops, do the rest of the shopping or tuck into freshly-made sweetmeats.

A favorite bazaar in New Delhi is the one held every Tuesday at Hanuman Mandir. It is also the city's biggest bangle market. Thousands of women visit the temple, then make tracks for the bangle sellers who dexterously slip on the tiniest glass bangles on to fat or slender wrists. The myriad colored bangles flecked with gold and silver, are worn to embellish and to draw out the colors of the sari or whatever traditional dress one wears. Glass bangles are considered auspicious and in Maharashtra and Uttar Pradesh green glass bangles are symbolic of marriage. On special occasions and festivals the women indulge themselves by buying bangles galore.

Every city has its version of "Chor Bazaar" or the market of stolen goods. Of course not all the goods here are stolen goods but the chances of recovering a stolen hubcap or the headlight of your favorite vintage car in Chor Bazaar are quite high! But apart from that the Chor Bazaar in Bombay offers a range of exquisite, antique artifacts, an elaborately carved wooden door or an ancient chandelier from a palace of yore — all for a song.

Indian handicrafts have a history and tradition that goes back many centuries. The finest artisans crafted for the king and his court. The less skilled catered to the needs of the common man. The five craftsmen available in the villages — the potter, the blacksmith, the carpenter, the weaver and the barber sustain the rural economy of contemporary India too. Knowledge and skill was communicated from father to son, from master to disciple. The craftsman was both designer and artisan and there was no dividing line between fine arts and crafts. An unusual degree of perfection was achieved in villages around temples because religious ritual demanded that only the fin-

Known as Arjuna's Penance and Penance of Bhagiratha, this stone sculpture at Mahabalipuram is the world's largest bas-relief at 25 meters by 6 meters. The panel depicting animals, deities and fables from the Panchatantra *is executed with great realism.*

est be offered to the gods.

The exquisite embroidery of Punjab, Gujarat and Rajasthan, the silks of Varanasi and Kanchipuram, the fine ivory carvings of Kerala, Uttar Pradesh and Delhi, the silver filigree work of Orissa, the bronze casting of Tanjore, sandalwood carving and sculpting of Mysore and the bamboo and cane work of the northeastern states are unique to India.

A friend who exports soft furnishings to half a dozen countries of the world including Japan found to her consternation that her Japanese business associates were turning up their noses when the baggage of neatly packed fabrics was opened up. They were objecting not to the fabrics or their finish but to the very Indian smell that they exuded ... a smell that had traveled thou-

sands of kilometers in sealed polythene bags. It was, they said, purely an "Indian" smell!

The anecdote best illustrates the lingering quality of the exotic smells, delicate fragrances and the aromatic flavors of India. From gardens on a summer night may emanate the heady fragrance of jasmines, often referred to as the "Queen of the Night" or other Indian flowers like the *champa* and the *madhumalti*.

In the Indian markets the sweet smell of mangoes and ripening guavas and the heady smell of ripe jackfruit blends with spices. In the temples there is the fragrance of incense

Nothing disturbs the serenity of the Golden Temple at Amritsar (left). Pilgrims do the parikram (circle of prayer and penance) round the holy sarovar. Humayun's tomb in Delhi (preceding pages) is the first substantial example of Mughal architecture.

Undoubtedly the king of Indian fruits, the mango can be found in fruit stalls all over India. There are hundreds of varieties and eating a mango with your hands without getting them messy is an art.

Nectar of the Gods

*A*sk anyone in India which their favorite fruit is, and almost without exception they will say mango. A mango ripened to the correct sweetness is food for the gods! There are mangoes and mangoes and mangoes and each variety has its own particular flavor and of course there are followers who swear by that particular species. A ripe mango need not necessarily be golden yellow or red. Delicious mangoes like the dussehri and langra (both these come from the state of Uttar Pradesh) are green. Experts can predict the ripeness of the mango just by the feel of the fruit and the texture of the skin. But the mango favored by foreign markets is the utterly delicious hapus or Alphonso that comes from the western state of Karnataka and Maharashtra, particularly from the district of Ratnagiri in Maharashtra. And it is not just foreigners who demand this variety of the fruit. Indians love its ambrosial flavor but the export market has pushed up prices and a single mango could cost as much as Rs 10 - 20 which they can ill afford.

The mango tree has special significance in rituals, specially on festival days. In southern India and in the west, mango leaves are strung into a garland and strung across doorways as an auspicious sign. All religious ceremonies have a kalasam *or small brass pot in which five leaves are arranged around the rim. A ripe mango is placed on the leaves. Gautama Buddha was presented a mango grove and often he would rest in the shade of the trees. So to Buddhists it is a sacred tree. Hindus consider it a reincarnation of Prajapati, the lord of all creatures. And mango wood is always used in funeral pyres.*

Many are the uses of the mango. The twigs are used as toothbrushes. The leaves are used in worship. The flowers are offered to the moon and to the Hindu equivalent of Cupid. And of course its shade is used by many a weary wanderer. The raw mango is used to make a delicious chutney, a chilled, delicious tall drink called "phool" or "pannah". It has excellent cooling properties. The ripe mango pulp is dried and packed in strips called "aam satto" in Bengali and "aam papad" anywhere in the north. Simply yummy.

But the mango tree is best loved by children during fruiting season, particularly when the mangoes are raw. Those who can't climb the higher reaches of the tree become expert markmen. They pick up stones and aim for the fruit and more often than not it drops! It is then cut up, spiced with salt and chilli powder and consumed! The teeth may get sour — but for the kids it's divine!

Aboard the Palace of Wheels, you can experience the romance of old-fashioned rail travel and relive the grandeur of a vanished era. From the ancient carriages of India has been created a train that combines old world charm with modern comforts.

Palace on Wheels

*I*t has been called *"the Taj Mahal of trains"*, India's magic and magnificent train", and "a splendor on the tracks", to mention just a few of the glowing adjectives used to describe the fabulous Palace on Wheels.

To travel on India's dream train is the ambition of all those who want to experience and enjoy the exotic. Instead of taking spaceships to unknown, uncharted destinations, on the Palace on Wheels you go backward into time, to the enchantment of an era that is a part of history.

Remnants of India's princely states and colonial raj have been put together for the ultimate in train luxury. As its name implies the Palace on Wheels is a collection of 13 vintage carriages, custom-made for the erstwhile maharajas, viceroys and governor-generals. It would take them cushioned and cocooned on hunting trips, to royal weddings, state visits and field inspections. Each of the regal saloons bears the insignia of the state to which it belonged.

For eight days this mobile miniature palace, pulled by an impressive black steam engine, takes you through 1,500 kilometers of green countryside interspersed with stretches of golden sand of the Thar desert. The Palace on Wheels operates only from October to April and takes you from Delhi Cantonment through the heartland of Rajasthan to Agra and the wondrous Taj Mahal.

There is no tiresome packing or unpacking at new hotels each day. Your palace hotel travels with you. Every morning luxury coaches pick you up from different railway stations to show you the city's attractions. You can relax in a swimming pool, wine and dine at a palace hotel, enjoy traditional music and dance and then return to your palace abode at the station where you are greeted with chilled handtowels to wipe off the day's weariness and dust.

Each coach accommodates eight persons and is equipped with two small toilet annex showers and a small elegant sitting room. In addition there is a separate dining car and a lounge-cum-library car with a well-stocked bar. On each coach are two personal attendants, turbaned Rajasthan-style, serving breakfast in bed or in the sitting room and fussing over the eight guests in true Indian style.

The living pageantry in which you are a participant includes elephant rides up to Amber fort in Jaipur and camel rides over the sand dunes of Jaisalmer at sunset. Dreaming of elephants and riding them in your sleep is supposed to be lucky and you fall asleep counting elephants to check on the veracity of the myth!

and wilting flowers that have to be ceremoniously disposed off in a holy river.

But undoubtedly the most exciting and mouth-watering aromas come from the Indian kitchens and the rich variety of its cuisines. Each region of the country has its own style of cooking and its own specialities. Continental and Chinese food with Indian flavors are additions to the country's culinary repertoire but the aromas that are wafted from Indian cooking have the taste buds yearning for traditional Indian dishes.

The food of Kashmir is predominantly Muslim but at the same time quite distinct from Muslim food from other parts of India. Lamb meat is extremely popular and is cooked in yoghurt, mustard oil and aniseeds. The Kashmir *biryani*, fragrant basmati rice cooked with tender mutton, spices and saffron is eaten with *roganjosh*, a sort of mutton stew simmered in a paste of red chilies, coriander, cummin, poppy seeds, cardamom, garlic, ginger and other ingredients.

South Indian cooking is noted for its extensive use of coconut and tamarind, both of which are readily available in the south. Rice is cooked a dozen different ways — the most exciting being lemon, coconut and tamarind rice.

There is an amazing variety of vegetables in the Indian market and a sizable section of the population is vegetarian. Proteins are acquired from lentils, pulses and dried beans like the moon bean, the red kidney bean and the black eyed bean which is cooked into a thick gravy.

Fish is popular in coastal towns where it is available in plenty. Everything from mackrel to sardines, red snapper, giant prawns, pomfrets and the Bombay duck are available and cooking them is an art in itself. Fish cooked in banana leaves over a charcoal flame has a special taste. If banana leaves are not easily available, aluminium foil may be used. In Bengal, fish is a must in every home and is cooked with mustard in mustard oil. Smoked *hilsa* is a gourmet's delight. In Kerala, fish cooked in coconut milk has its own flavor.

The Mughals added opulence to classical

The old city of Srinagar, nestling on the river Jhelum, has its own mystique and charm. It is as pretty at sunset as it is in the daytime when the shikara *gondalas ply by giving tourists their first tantalizing glimpse of the city.*

Indian cuisine particularly in Uttar Pradesh. The *shammi* and *seekh* kebabs are made from minced meat spiced lightly and fried in the form of small cutlets or barbecued over a charcoal fire.

Unlike in the west, cooking and eating is an elaborate ritual and a fine art. Great emphasis is placed on freshly cooked food and canned and frozen food is frowned upon. In fact in many homes, spices are freshly

off as though they are Sanskrit *slokas* or verses and old and young alike hum their favorite film songs. Though video and television have made inroads into cinema, 700 to 800 films are still churned out every year.

India is today the biggest producer of films in the world making twice the number produced in Hollywood. Though the films are made in 16 Indian dialects, Hindi films dominate the celluloid scene.

ground before use. Most meals are still eaten with the fingers to get the full joy of eating, and licking the fingers is most definitely recommended!

However hard you may try to concentrate on the maddening, slow-moving traffic of the metropolis your attention is drawn to the huge film billboards and hoardings stuck on flyovers, bridges, lampposts and even on the outer walls of temples. Favorite actors and actresses in vulgar poses look down on a film-crazy public.

In India, films are the cheapest form of entertainment. Filmy dialogues are rattled

Film stars are worshiped like demi-gods and their popularity makes it easy for them to enter politics. India had its own film-star-turned politician long before Ronald Reagan became President of the USA. Tamil film hero, MG Ramachandran, was until his death recently, the chief minister of Tamil Nadu. Mr NTR Ram Rao, who played the role of gods in Telugu films is firmly installed as chief minister of Andhra Pradesh. Amitabh Bachchan, whose handsome face leers at you from most hoardings, had acted in over 60 films when he took to politics.

Melodrama, violence, sex, sentimentality and of course, a lot of songs — these are the ingredients of "masala" or popular film. The world of make-believe and romance provides three hours of undiluted escapism for the poor, the oppressed

Once a year at Id Milan, the Taj Mahal comes alive as thousands gather to worship and renew ties of brotherhood (right). At Sikandra, 25 kilometers from Agra, is Akbar's tomb (above). Built by his son Jahangir, it combines Muslim and Hindu architectural styles.

and those struggling out of the morass of middle class anonymity.

But it is not all sex and violence. Some excellent art films are produced too. The "new wave" films as they are called are powerful, moving and a reflection as well as satire on modern society. They don't do too well at the box office but more people are sitting up and taking note of them and many are winning international awards.

India's Satyajit Ray has the same status as Bergman, John Houston and Kurosawa. Following in his footsteps are Govind Nihlani, Shyam Benegal, Basu Bhattacharya, Arvindam, Girish Karnad and Adoor Gopalakrishnan.

A time may come when if someone asks "What shall I bring you from abroad?" you have to think twice. Because almost everything is made in India from safety pins to aeroplanes.

Though it was India's first Prime Minister, Jawaharlal Nehru, who sought to use technology for eliminating hunger and

A sadhu at the Kumbh Mela fair at Allahabad reaches for some holy ashes to cover his body (above). Jain munis or sadhus of a particular sect, who do not wear clothes for fear of harming living creatures, hold discourse (right).

poverty, it is his grandson, Rajiv Gandhi, who wants to take India into the twenty-first century with the help of science and technology.

Next to the Soviet Union and the USA, India has the largest stock of technological manpower and is among the first ten industrial countries of the world. Indian engineers, doctors and scientists have made positive contributions the world over. Dr

With its sights set on the stars, India has entered the space age. At the Vikram Sarabhai space center at Trivandrum, rockets and satellites and their instrumentation and propellants are manufactured and from the Thumba equatorial rocket station they soar into space. Scientists from several countries are working with Indian scientists at Thumba.

The first Indian satellite, Aryabhatta, was

Hargovind Khorana, a naturalized American, is a Nobel prize winner for his work on genetics.

Steel mills at Durgapur, Rourkela and Bhilai keep the wheels of industry churning and nuclear plants at Trombay (outside Bombay), Narora (in Haryana), and Kalpakkam (near Madras) and Kotah (in Rajasthan) are helping India stay abreast in agriculture and medicine. Radio isotopes are exported as well as used locally for diagnosis and medical therapy. On the agriculture front they are being used to develop high yielding and disease-resistant strains of wheat and rice. The power generated from the thermal stations is insufficient for increasing population and .mushrooming industries and nuclear power is being tapped at five atomic stations.

put into orbit in 1975 and since then seven indigenous satellites have been launched. Weather forecasting as well as telecommunication satellites (INSATS) have also been put into orbit with US assistance. India's own telecommunication satellite and 180 television transmitters have made it possible to beam classroom work to remote villages. Children who have never seen a film are fascinated by the pictures and images on the community set. Farmers, too, tune on to special programs to improve their knowledge about fertilisers, crop rotation and high yielding varieties. India's

India is the birthplace of many religions. At Bodh Gaya, where the Buddha received enlightenment, devotees flock to the shrine to ask for blessings (above). In Sravanabelagola, the giant statue of Lord Bahubali (left) draws Jain pilgrims from all over India.

new goal is to provide television facilities to the over 500,000 villages in which seventy per cent of its population still lives.

The space odyssey achieved new heights with Rakesh Sharma becoming the first Indian to go into space on a Soviet Soyuz T-11. In keeping with Indian traditions Sharma performed yogic exercises to counter weightlessness.

More recently India has joined a select

band of countries — the Soviet Union, the United States, France and Japan — which have their own remote sensing satellite. Now with its "eye in the sky" India can manage its natural resources better than ever before.

But modernization has not changed the people, their warmth, hospitality and effusiveness. Unlike in the west visitors are brought home to share a meal which the housewife or her domestic help has spent hours cooking. Little children address you "uncle" or "aunty" out of respect and affection. It is as though you have been accepted into the extended Indian family.

Whether you see it in the distance as the backdrop of the brown, barren fields (left), or from close quarters like these young visitors (above),the Taj is ever magnificent. Built by the Mughal emperor Shah Jahan, it is the world's most enduring monument to love.

Back of the Book

This section provides detailed information and interesting insights that will enhance your trip to India. The maps depict the Indian subcontinent, its location, the country's principal cities and towns and physical characteristics. Suggested sightseeing itineraries accompanied by regional maps help you get around India's prime tourist towns and attractions and be a witness to India's fabulous landmarks, fascinating historical sites and splendid wildlife sanctuaries. Best Bets is a digest of some of the more interesting things India has to offer, from antiques to camel safaris. .Finally, the Travel Notes summarize the essential basic information needed to make a visit to India successful and enjoyable.

*Though the princely states were wound up half a century ago, royal customs are still practiced on special occasions. At Jaipur an elephant's legs are painted over in the most exquisite designs and colors (**left**) as it is readied for a royal procession.*

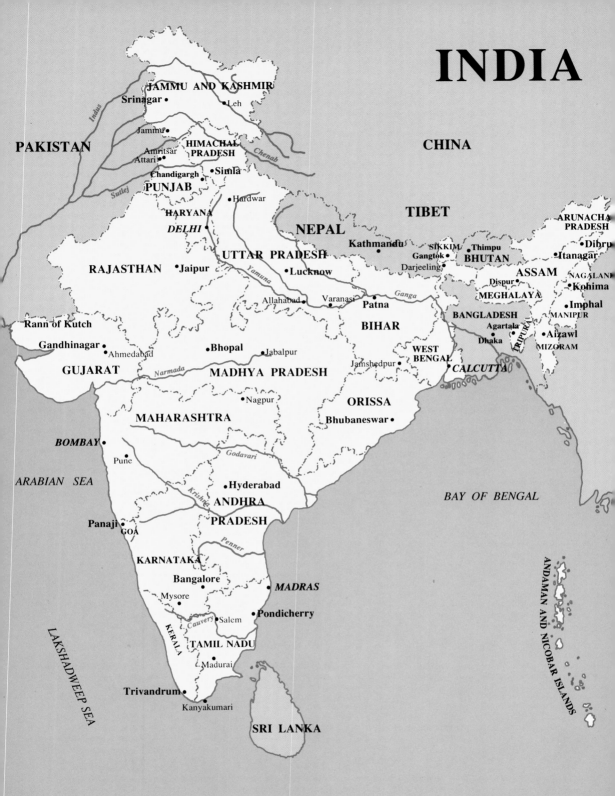

INDIA

PAKISTAN

CHINA

JAMMU AND KASHMIR
Srinagar
Leh
Jammu
Indus
HIMACHAL
Amritsar PRADESH
Attari
Chandigargh Simla
PUNJAB
HARYANA
Hardwar
DELHI
Chenab
Sutlej

TIBET

ARUNACHAL
PRADESH

RAJASTHAN
Jaipur

UTTAR PRADESH
Lucknow
NEPAL
Kathmandu
Yamuna
Allahabad Varanasi
Patna
BIHAR

SIKKIM
Gangtok Thimpu
Darjeeling BHUTAN
Ganga

Dibru
Itanagar

ASSAM
Dispur
MEGHALAYA
NAGALAND
Kohima

Rann of Kutch
Gandhinagar
Ahmedabad
Bhopal Jabalpur
GUJARAT
Narmada
MADHYA PRADESH

WEST
BENGAL
CALCUTTA

BANGLADESH
Agartala
Dhaka
TRIPURA

Imphal
MANIPUR
Aizawl
MIZORAM

Nagpur
MAHARASHTRA
ORISSA
Bhubaneswar

Jamshedpur

BOMBAY
Pune
Godavari

ARABIAN SEA

Hyderabad
ANDHRA
Krishna
PRADESH
Panaji
GOA
Penner

BAY OF BENGAL

KARNATAKA
Bangalore
Mysore
MADRAS
Pondicherry
Cauvery Salem

ANDAMAN AND NICOBAR ISLANDS

LAKSHADWEEP SEA

KERALA
TAMIL NADU
Madurai
Trivandrum
Kanyakumari

SRI LANKA

INDIAN OCEAN

The Northern Region

DELHI. Delhi is history — ancient history as well as the unfolding story of modern, democratic India. It has been the seat of power of seven empires, each of which has left its distinctive mark in the form of monuments and architecture. Plundering armies of Timur the Lame and Nadir Shah have ravaged and ransacked the city in the 14th and 18th centuries carrying away the famous Kohinoor diamond and the magnificent peacock throne.

But Delhi was invincible. Out of its ruins and ashes emerged a new strength and yet another empire. Both New Delhi built by Edwin Lutyens and the British and Old Delhi built by earlier rulers including that Mughal master builder, Shah Jahan, is replete with monuments. Almost every street and locality has some history — the remnants of an ancient wall, a mosque or a tomb. On the ruins of seven cities stands the pulsating, vibrant capital of today.

The foundation of Dhillika, from which has emerged the new name Delhi — the first of the seven medieval cities, was laid by the Tomars, Rajput chieftains in the 8-9th century AD, in the area in South Delhi known as Lalkot. Around the middle of the 12th century it was conquered by the Chauhans and Prithiviraj Chauhan extended it and added a second line of fortification now called Qila Rai Pithora. In 1290, the Khilji sultanate came to power and they established Siri, the second city of Delhi close to Hauz Khas. The Tughluqs raised the third city of Delhi called Tughlaqabad, eight kilometers to the south of Lalkot. The fourth city, Jahanpanah, and the fifth, Firuzabad were built by the later Tughluqs. The Saiyads and Lodis also ruled in Delhi but did not add very much to the existing architecture and buildings.

The first Mughal emperor in India, Babur, had his capital in Agra. It was the second Mughal emperor, Humayun, who built the sixth capital, Din Panah at the site of the Purana Qila. The fifth Mughal emperor, Shah Jahan, built an extremely well-planned township, Shahjahanabad the seventh city, with the Red Fort as its citadel. Most of Shahjahanabad has stayed intact and is today the hub of trade and business. Its labyrinthine lanes and streets, each devoted to a particular trade, are fascinating though strangers could get lost.

Delhi once again became the capital in December 1911 under the British. A sandstone pillar at Kingsway Camp in North Delhi is mute testimony to the durbar that was held here on the visit of King George V and Queen Mary. British statues that once adorned important intersections and

buildings have been dumped in this graveyard of the British raj.

But the more enduring of the British buildings that have given New Delhi a very distinct character are **Rashtrapati Bhavan**, the official residence of India's President on Raisina Hill with its 340 rooms and extensive lawns, the **Central Secretariat** and **Parliament House**. **India Gate**, the memorial arch of the first World War, is the center point of Delhi. It is comparable to London's Trafalgar Square, the Eiffel Tower of Paris and Washington Monument in Washington DC. Between Rashtrapati Bhavan and India Gate are held the processions, the demonstrations and the pageantry of a highly political city.

Connaught Place, the double-storied market place built by the British in the shape of an enormous circle is also distinctive despite the skyscrapers that have come up on its outer periphery.

New Delhi is India's garden city. Residential areas are interspersed with well laid-out parks and lawns. Since independence the city has grown at a tremendous pace — its urban sprawl reaching out to the fringes of neighboring cities. The New Delhi of today is larger and bigger in area than all the previous seven cities put together.

There is so much to see and do in Delhi that even a week is often not enough. To get a flavor of the city you could do a round of some of the monuments, spend half a day browsing in the city of Shahjahan, now called Chandni Chowk, and do the museum and art galleries. No visit to Delhi is complete without a visit to the **Birla Mandir**, where thousands come to worship, and a walk in at least one or two of Delhi's gardens. Highly recommended are the Budha Jayanti Park in West Delhi and the Lodi Gardens in South Delhi.

Other sights well worth visiting are:

Purana Qila. Located seven kilometers south of the heart of the city, the remains of this ancient fort, built by Sher Shah Suri (1538-1545) contain the ruins of Indraprastha, the ancient 3rd-4th century BC city of the Pandavas — heroes of the *Mahabharata*, the national epic of India.

Parts of the two-kilometer irregular oblong wall have disappeared but it is still an imposing structure and a prominent landmark of New Delhi. There are three impressive gates leading to Purana Qila, double-storied, built with red sandstone and mounted with "chhatris" or umbrella-like constructions. But only the main gate near the Delhi Zoo is in use. It is believed that Sher Shah Suri left Purana Qila incomplete and it

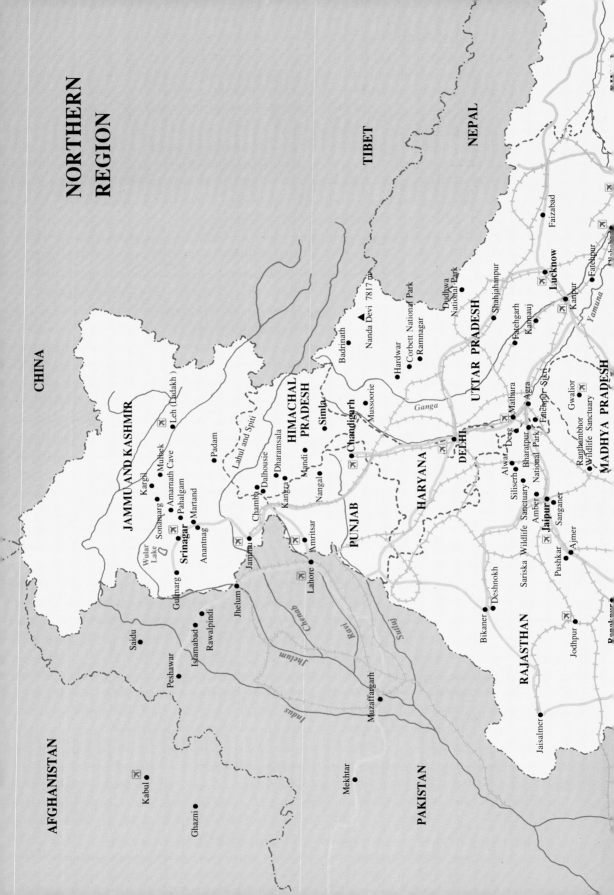

was completed by Emperor Humayun.

Qutb Minar. The highest tower in India, the Qubt Minar lies some eleven kilometers south of New Delhi. The construction of this 72.5-meter tall victory tower cum minaret to call the faithful to pray at the adjoining mosque was started by Qutb-ud-din Aibak in 1199 and completed by Iltutmish Alauddin who is said to have added the Alai Darwaza or gateway on its southern complex. A pleasant half day can be spent at the Qutb complex and the surrounding Mehrauli and Tughluqabad areas.

Humayun's Tomb. One of Delhi's finest monuments, Humayun's tomb is located 1.5 kilometers south of the city. Built in the mid-16th century by Haji Begum, wife of the second Mughal emperor, Humayun, this tomb is said to be the precursor to the Taj Mahal at Agra. Its high arched entrances, bulbous dome and the formal gardens surrounding have been refined in the magnificent Taj. Humayun's wife is also buried in the complex.

Hazrat Nizam-ud-din Aulia. Almost opposite Humayun's tomb is the shrine of the Muslim saint Nizam-ud-din Aulia. The original tomb has disappeared without a trace. The present structure was constructed almost 240 years later in 1562. The Nizam-ud-din complex is extremely interesting and on the pilgrim route of the Muslims. Twice a year, on the death anniversaries of Nizam-ud-din Aulia and his chief disciple, Amir Khusro, also a celebrated saint and poet, the entire area comes alive with pilgrims from all over congregating here. The tombs of the poet-saint, Jahanara, Shah Jahan's elder daughter, Muhammad Shah and Mirza Jahangir, the eldest son of Akbar, all descendants of the great Mughal rulers, are also in this area.

Jama Masjid. Just south of Chandni Chowk it is the largest mosque in India with a capacity to receive 25,000 pilgrims at a time. It is also said to be the final architectural extravaganza of Shah Jahan. Built with red sandstone and white marble it has three gateways, four angle towers and two minarets which stand 40 meters high. An impressive flight of steps leads to the Masjid proper. The mosque was used by both the emperor and his subjects, the upper storey over the eastern gateway being used by royalty. The mosque has undergone considerable repairs.

Red Fort or Lal Qila. Situated on the west bank of the Yamuna this fort made of red sandstone as its name denotes, symbolizes the zenith of Mughal power and majesty. It was constructed by Shah Jahan over a six-year period though he never completely moved his capital from Agra to Delhi. The fort is situated off one of the busiest thoroughfares of Delhi. On entering the fort the noise of the city disappears and peace prevails.

The Indian army occupies parts of this historic monument today but there is plenty to see. At the **Diwan-i-Am** (Hall of Public Audience) the emperor would sit in an alcove in the wall, marble-panelled and set with precious stones, to hear the complaints of his subjects. The precious stones were gouged out during the Mutiny but this elegant hall was later repaired by Lord Curzon.

Also in the Red Fort, just north of the Diwan-i-Am is the Hall of Private Audience or **Diwan-i-Khas**. Here Shah Jahan sat in all his splendor on the famous peacock throne which in 1739 was carted off by Nadir Shah. Inscribed on the wall of the hall is a Persian couplet: "If there is paradise on earth it is this, it is this."

Other interesting features of the Red Fort are the royal baths with domes, the **Moti Masjid** or Pearl Mosque made of sparkling marble by Aurangzeb in 1659, the **Rang Mahal** or "painted palace" and the **Khas Mahal**, the private palace of the emperor.

Part of that glory, that history is recreated every evening through a sound-and-light show which introduces tourists to the rich and complex history of the Mughals. The fort was witness not only to Mughal splendor but to the fight for India's independence and the historic unfurling of the Indian tricolour on August 15, 1947. Even today on the anniversary of that day the Prime Minister addresses the nation from these historic ramparts.

Museum Tour. Among the many museums in Delhi worth a visit are the National Museum of Janpath with its fine collection of Indian bronzes, terracotta and wood sculptures dating back to the Mauryan period; Nehru Museum, the official residence of the first Indian Prime Minister with items and documents relating to his life; the Rail Museum at Chanakyapuri which has a fascinating collection of old engines, including one of 1855 in working order; the International Dolls Museum which has several thousand dolls from 85 countries; the Crafts Museum at the Pragati Maidan exhibition grounds eight kilometers from Connaught Place which with its mud huts and bullock carts recreates the rural ambience in the heart of New Delhi.The Crafts Museum has demonstrations and displays of traditional Indian crafts in textiles, metal, wood and ceramics.

Upcountry

AGRA. Well connected by road and rail to Delhi is Agra, the city that has been put on the international map by the great Mughals. It is a crowded city on the banks of the river Yamuna with bustling alleys and an unending stream of rickshaws. It is well known for its leather industry, inlay work in marble, *petha* (pumpkin sweet) and *dal moth* (fried salted chickpeas). But it is the wealth of historical monuments that brings thousands of tourists to Agra every month.

No one who comes to Delhi goes back without seeing Agra, 203 kilometers south of Delhi. There are deluxe buses, a good train service, the Taj Express and tourist taxis that get you there in under four hours. Its main attractions include:

Agra Fort. Built by the greatest of the Mughal emperors, Akbar, between 1565-1573 the fort is located on the bend of the Yamuna river almost in the center of the city. The imposing fort made of red sandstone was occupied by three great Mughal emperors — Akbar, Jahangir and Shah Jahan, each of whom made contributions to this mighty citadel. It was here in Musamman Burj that Shah Jahan died in captivity gazing at his creation, the Taj Mahal. Like the Red Fort at Delhi, the Agra Fort has halls of audience, ornamental bathing house, Moti Masjid (Pearl Mosque), Machchhi Bhawan (palace with fish tanks) and an excellent vineyard.

Taj Mahal. The mausoleum of the Empress Mumtaz Mahal who died in 1630 has been called "a dream in marble" and an "irridescent dream of a love-lorn emperor". It took Shah Jahan 18 years to build this exquisite marble monument.

Within the Taj complex is a forecourt, a charming garden in the Mughal style with canals and a central tank with fountains, the tomb itself, an attached mosque on the west and its counterpart on the east. The perfect symmetry in architecture — the tapering minarets balanced on the four corners of the main octagonal edifice, the onion-shaped dome have sent architects as well as poets into raptures. The graves of both Mumtaz Mahal and her lover Shah Jahan are in the crypt and above them in the main chamber are the false tombs more magnificent than their subterranean counterparts. With an amazing variety of precious gems, the mosaic work adorning the cenotaphs is said to be the finest in the world.

At the mosque, adjacent to the main mausoleum, prayers are still held. Every full moon night and the four nights preceding and following, it is open till midnight. To enjoy the beauty of this marble masterpiece you should visit it at different times of the day.

Itmad-ud-Daulah. Across the Yamuna is the tomb of Jahangir's prime minister, Ghyas Beg, the father of his beloved consort Nur Jahan. Nur Jahan's mother is also buried here. A forerunner to the Taj Mahal, the tomb was built by the Empress Nur Jahan between 1622 and 1628. It is a square marble building with four corner towers and a canopy-shaped roof. The workmanship is extremely fine, almost like lace. Itmad-ud-Daulah has its own ardent admirers many of whom feel it is as beautiful as the Taj.

Sikandra. The tomb of Emperor Akbar in a spacious garden enclosed with high wall is in a locality named after Sikandar Lodi. Like the Taj and Itmad-ud-Daulah it is decorated with four minarets. Though Akbar began the construction of the tomb in a spacious garden, it is Jahangir who made some alterations in the original design before completing it.

FATEHPUR SIKRI. Akbar's capital for 12 years, Fatehpur Sikri is the ruins of his imperial city, 36 kilometers west of Agra. The red sandstone structures of the city are enclosed in a wall which is 11 kilometers in circumference. Saint Salim Chishti whose remains lie in Fatehpur Sikri, had prophesied that Sikri would be auspicious for the emperor. This was also the center from where Akbar carried out his experiments in art and architecture. The design combines architectural styles of India, Central Asia and Iran. The sprawling Fatehpur complex includes the palace of Akbar's Hindu wife, Jodhabai, the ornate house of the legendary quick-witted courtier Birbal and the Jami Masjid. The entrance is through a monumental gateway called Buland Darwaza.

VARANASI. From Delhi there are flights as well as trains to Varanasi, known as the "eternal city" and the "city of Shiva". In the scriptures it is "Kashi", an important pilgrim center. To die at Varanasi and be cremated at the famous Manikarnika ghats is the dream of the devout Hindus.

So thousands of them, particularly widows, come to spend their last years at Varanasi. With its quaint, crowded alleys, all leading to the long row of ghats (steps with a landing) on the river front, Varanasi has become a major tourist attraction. It is here that you can feel the religious pulse of India, its spirituality and the people's implicit faith in destiny. It has also been the center for Hindu learning and culture and the Benaras (the old name

of Varanasi) Hindu University continues to be a premier educational institute of the country.

The best time to visit the ghats is before the pink lights of dawn touch the skies. Towed to the river front on a cycle rickshaw along with umpteen others in the traditional means of transport you will see ghostly figures stealthily walking down the steps to the waterfront. At dawn, when the sun rises there will be hundreds of devotees bathing in the river, worshiping the sun and cleansing their souls of sin in the holy waters of the Ganga River.

A boat ride down the river at dusk is equally rewarding. The flames of a myriad funeral pyres are slowly dying, seagulls head homewards and little children swim between boats and dive in to get the coins thrown into the river.

Among the other historical places to visit in Varanasi are the mosque of Aurangzeb, the Durga Temple, the modern Tulsi Manas Temple, Ramnagar Fort, the 17th century home of the former ruling Maharaja which houses a museum of brocades, silver and palanquins, and the new Vishvanath Temple built by the industrialists — the Birlas.

Just a half-hour drive from Varanasi is **Sarnath** where Lord Buddha delivered his first sermon after attaining enlightenment. Among the remains at Sarnath are the Dhamekh stupa, the main shrine, and an Ashokan pillar.

JAIPUR. Ask any tourist which places he plans to visit in India and almost without exception Jaipur is one of the places on the itinerary. Jaipur is the city of princes and princesses, of tales of valor and courage, of romance and chivalry.

The capital of Rajasthan, Jaipur like Agra, is just a four-hour drive from Delhi. Rajasthan is India at its colorful best. It is not only the rich-hued turbans of the men, the striking swirling skirts of the women and their colorful accessories that add to the enchantment of Rajasthan but the endless stretches of desert sand, the glittering palaces that have been turned into hotels and the many feasts and festivals of its people.

If you split up the word "Rajasthan" into Raja and Sthan, literally translated it means "the Land of King". When India became independent some 23 princely states merged to form Rajasthan. The Rajputs or the warrior class which reigned supreme for a thousand years in this area had the chivalry and the code of conduct of the medieval knights of Europe. "Do or die" was their motto.

Jaipur is known as the Pink City but it was not always this color. The original Japur is said to have been painted gray with white borders and

motifs. But just before Prince Albert, consort of Queen Victoria, visited India in 1883 it was painted pink, the traditional color of welcome and this has since been retained.

Two Jaipur buildings you should not miss are the City Palace and the Palace of Winds.

City Palace. The Jaipur family lives in a part of this palace but the museum section is open to visitors. Several gates lead to the palace but it's best to enter through the Court of Justice and the Jantar Mantar Observatory of Maharaja Jai Singh 11. The City Palace has an excellent collection of textiles, carpets, paintings, manuscripts and arms. On display is the giant silver vessel in which the maharaja used to take drinking water with him to England — "foreign" water was thought to be tainted!

Palace of Winds. This honeycomb-like five-story building in the heart of Jaipur is known as Hawa Mahal or the Palace of Winds. It was built in 1799 by Maharaja Sawai Pratap Singh for the royal ladies of his family. Traditionally ladies, particularly of the royal family, were heavily veiled in public so they couldn't see much of what was going on around them. Once the Hawa Mahal was built, these ladies could sit behind the delicate stone friezes and watch everyday life go by! Today only the facade of the building remains but if you climb to the top of the building you can get an excellent view of Jaipur.

AMBER. Eleven kilometers from Jaipur on the Jaipur-Delhi road is the ancient capital of Jaipur state. This fortress-palace was constructed by Raja Man Singh, the commander of Akbar's army, in the late sixteenth century. The fort, a good example of Rajput architecture, stands on a hill summit overlooking the town and a lake.

A great attraction today is the elephant ride to the top of the fort. Caparisoned and painted elephants march up and down the steep slope and very often a *sarangi*, a stringed instrument player, serenades you through the ride. A visit to Sheesh Mahal (Palace of Mirrors) is an unforgetable experience. Several Indian films have been made in the setting of Sheesh Mahal. If you light a match in this palace of mirrors, it comes aglow with a hundred lights reflected from each piece of glass.

SANGANER. For those who are interested in ancient art, culture and history there is a ruined palace and the finely carved Jain temples. But those who wish to see a vibrant and modern Sanganer must visit the area of the block printers. These delicate, attractive designs for textiles, parti-

cularly saris, draw visitors in thousands from all over the country.

BHARATPUR. A well-known spot on the world heritage map this 29-square kilometer wetland bird sanctuary is a definite stopover for rare migratory birds like the Siberian Crane. Known as the Keoladeo Ghana Sanctuary, thousands of birds can be seen here, particularly from October to March. Bharatpur can be reached from Jaipur and is just 55 kilometers from Agra.

At one time Bharatpur was the duck shooting preserve of the Maharajas of Bharatpur. One recorded shoot toted up 4,273 birds on a single day! Hunting was stopped in 1964.

Thirty kilometers from Bharatpur is the wonderful Deeg Palace, set on the water's edge with cool channels, fountains and water alleys below. The Maharaja of Bharatpur is said to have attacked the Red Fort at Delhi at one stage and carried off an entire marble building which can now be seen at Deeg.

SARISKA. This wildlife sanctuary is 107 kilometers from Jaipur and 200 kilometers from Delhi. The 480-square kilometer sanctuary nestles in a valley surrounded by green and brown hills. Equipped with flashlights, a ride through the sanctuary after sunset can show up an amazing range of animal activity. At Sariska, tigers, leopards, neelgai (blue bull), spotted deer and wild boar can be seen.

PUSHKAR. Just 11 kilometers from Ajmer, Pushkar is an important place of pilgrimage for the Hindus. On a November full moon every year it comes alive with one of the country's biggest cattle fairs. The town clings to the side of a beautiful lake which has many bathing ghats. There are not many temples in India to Brahma, the Creator, but Pushkar has one. The Pushkar Fair at night resembles a fairyland with little earthern lamps and men and women in their colorful best seeking the blessings of the Lord.

It is not difficult to find cheap lodgings at Pushkar. For those looking for the exotic, a palace has been converted into a lodging house. Sunsets over the lake at Pushkar are nothing short of spectacular.

JAISALMER. This desert outpost of Rajasthan has been described by ecstatic tourists as "a living museum" and "a golden city". But it is something more than just that. It seems like a place from a fairy tale. Centuries ago, Jaisalmer was on the ancient trade route linking India with the trading centers of Central Asia. This brought wealth and prosperity to the people of Jaisalmer who displayed their riches by building exquisite houses and mansions (*havelis*) all carved from the region's yellow sandstone. The palace, the temples in the fort, and even the shops have been fashioned from this yellow stone that gives the golden aura to Jaisalmer. All modern constructions have to be of the same stone or hue so that the old and the new blend with one another.

The old city is surrounded by a fort wall and within this rises a hill with more fortified walls. The inner citadel of the fort crowns the Trikuta Hill and inside this enclosure can be found a group of finely carved Jain temples that date from the 12th to the 15th century.

The development of shipping routes, the opening up of Bombay port and ultimately the partition of India which cut off the trade route through Pakistan led to the decline of Jaisalmer. It is only in the last 10 to 15 years that it is being developed as a tourist center.

KASHMIR. Kashmir is paradise. It is three worlds really — Jammu the home of the Dogras with its temples beckoning pilgrims from every part of India; the Valley — a dream garden with houseboats plying on the placid waters of Dal Lake, and Ladakh, closer to heaven with its moonscape-like terrain and monasteries peering down from rocky heights. Each season has something to offer. Spring comes in gentle, pastel shades — pink, blue and white. In summer the valley is a sea of a myriad colors and blossoms. Come autumn and the fruit trees groan with the apples, peaches and apricots on their slender branches. The chinar trees change their colors taking on red and golden hues. Winter covers the valley and Ladakh with a blanket of snow. Solitude descends. Only the snow-laden higher slopes are throbbing with activity as skiers make merry on the snow.

There are daily flights from Delhi to Srinagar, the capital, and the trains come up to Jammu. From there to the valley it is a superb drive.

JAMMU. Jammu has been called the Gateway to the Valley. According to legend, King Jambulochan saw a tiger and a goat drinking water from the same pool and considering this auspicious he laid the foundations of the present city.

Jammu is the winter capital of the state but it is more famous for its temples and the endless trek of pilgrims to Vaishnodevi, 48 kilometers from the city near Katra.

Raghunath temples in the middle of the city have a profusion of fascinating marble sculptures

of different colors and gigantic proportions. There are also some exquisite wall paintings in some of the temples.

Amar Mahal Palace is the tallest structure in Jammu and a marvel of architecture designed by a French architect for Raja Amar Singh. The palace is on a hillock overlooking the Tawi river. The palace now houses a rare collection of Pahari paintings and family portraits of the ruling family of the city. Old Dogra art and Pahari paintings can also be seen at the Dogra Art Gallery near the New Secretariat.

SRINAGAR. A network of waterways laces the city together and life flows alongside it. Like Swiss chalets, many houses seem to be hanging over the lake from the surrounding hills. But the old parts of the city is quite different with houses stacked on the narrow streets. Srinagar is famous for its Mughal style gardens, Dal and Nagin lakes with their comfortable *shikara* or row boats and the endless variety of its handicrafts.

Hazratbal. On the shores of Dal Lake, this mosque houses one of the holiest Muslim relics — a hair of prophet Muhammad. The precious hair was brought to Kashmir from Bijapur by Khwaja Noor-ud-din in 1700. On specific days in the year it is shown to the faithful who come from all over the country.

Mughal Gardens. These exquisite gardens were laid out four centuries ago by the Mughal emperors for their rest and relaxation. With fountains sending up spools of rose-scented water, large channels of water and a myriad flowers arranged in set color patterns, there was a magical quality to the gardens. No longer are the fountain waters scented but the gardens have retained to a large measure their character.

Shalimar and Nishat, further down Boulevard Road, have a symmetrical pattern of garden terraces, waterways and fountains. Nishat is the larger garden with an impressive plantation of chinars. Shalimar is more popular because it is here that the famous romance of Nur Jahan and Jahangir was enacted. A sound-and-light show in English and Urdu retells the legendary romance every evening in the tourist season.

Daily excursions to Nagin Lake, Wular Lake and Manasbal Lake can be made. With sailing, swimming and water-skiing facilities, Nagin Lake is paradise for those interested in aquatic activities. Wular is the largest freshwater lake in Asia. It is surrounded by mountains and in the middle of the jade green waters is a picturesque island,

Zaina Lank, which has an ancient mosque with elegant pillars and arches rising from its ruins. Manasbal is a bird lovers' delight. Covered with lotus blossoms this small lake is home to hundreds of birds in summer.

Kashmir is famous for its handicrafts such as papier-mâché, lacquered and painted in floral designs, walnut woodcarvings, an array of carpets, "toosh" shawls that are so fine and soft that they can go through a ring, exquisitely embroidered shawls and linen and of course soft silks. Several semi-precious stones can also be purchased at Srinagar.

LADAKH. From Srinagar there are deluxe as well as ordinary buses through Kargil to Leh, the capital of Ladakh. Kargil at 2,740 meters is 204 kilometers from Srinagar.

Though most tourists go to Leh, the capital and principal township of Ladakh, and the famous monasteries around it — Shey, Sankar, Phyang, Spituk and Hemis, few trek to the interior villages of the Nubra Valley or the Zanskar region. The western flank of Ladakh comprise several valleys that are still untainted by tourism. It is only the intrepid trekker who venture into and enjoy the unsullied beauty of Drass, Suru, Mulbekh and Zanskar. In the winter months the Srinagar-Leh road is snowbound. Those seeking to visit these Himalayan abode of the Gods should do so in the summer months.

Kargil is the second largest city of Ladakh. Once on the caravan route of traders from China, Turkey and Afghanistan, Kargil today is a quiet town. Visible all round the little township are lush green fields of barley and wheat, vegetable beds and rows upon rows of poplars and willows. Kargil is famous for its apricots and mulberries.

From Kargil daylong excursions to Mulbekh or Suru valley give a splendid view of the Himalayas from close quarters. Mulbekh, 45 kilometers from Kargil, is a small Buddhist village. Many monuments of the early Buddhist era dot the landscape. A major attraction of the village is the nine-meter rock sculpture of Maitreya, the future Buddha. The Mulbekh *gompa* (monastery) dominates the valley and is adorned with frescoes and statues.

Five kilometers from Mulbekh is Shergole, another monastery that literally hangs out from the brown granite of the rocks. Urgyan Rzong is a meditational retreat tucked behind a natural mountain fortress. Senior Buddhist monks perform penance in isolation in the caves here. The only approach to the caves is a narrow pathway.

WESTERN & CENTRAL REGION

BAY OF BENGAL

ARABIAN SEA

MADHYA PRADESH

Mirzapur
Ramnagar
Champa
Mankpur
Satna
Bhandavgarh National Park
Raipur
ORISSA
Chhatarpur
Khajuraho
Jabaipur
Kanha National Park
Bhilai
Durg
Jagdalpur
Lalitpur
Chander
Sagar
Pachmari
Chhindwara
Nagpur
Tadoba National Park
Chandrapur
Palampet
Warangal
Rajahmundry
Godavari
Bhopal
Agar
Khandwa
Akot
Khammam
ANDHRA PRADESH
Narmada
Ujjain
Indore
Burhanpur
Ajanta Caves
Daulatabad
Nizamabad
Secunderabad
Srisailam
Kota
Mandu
Ellora
Aurangabad
Paithan
Hyderabad
Chittorgarh
Udaipur
MAHARASHTRA
Osmanabad
Bidaro
Barsi
KARNATAKA
Hampi
Hospet
Gandhinagar
Vadodara
Saputara
Nasik
Bhimashankar
Karla Caves
Mahabaleshwar
Bijapur
Belgaum
Ahmedabad
Surat
Silvassa
Bhiwandi
Pune
Sangli
Dharwad
Patan
Modhera
Lothal
Daman (G D & D)
Karnala
Panhala
GOA
Panaji
Bhavnagar
Palitana
Bombay
Elephanta
Murud
Ratnagiri
Dabolim
(Goa Daman & Diu)
Rajkot
Keshod
DIU (G D & D)
GUJARAT
Bhuj
Kandla
Jamnagar
Somnath
Porbandar
Dwarka

The Western and Central Region

BOMBAY. With a busy international airport as well as a harbor receiving ships from far and near, Bombay is India's business center — its economic powerhouse and industrial hub. Everything from cars and textiles to pharmaceuticals are manufactured in this city situated on India's west coast.

Because of its tall, imposing skyscrapers it has been called the "Manhattan of India". The unending stream of films churned out from its 12 studios and the actors and actresses living in its exclusive, elite areas have earned it yet another title — the Hollywood of India. From all parts of the country people rush to Bombay with dreams of wealth and glory. The tremendous population pressure is manifest in the slums that come up in the poshest areas of Bombay and the large number of pavement dwellers.

Yet in the early 16th century Bombay was just a conglomeration of seven islands occupied largely by the fisher folk called Kolis. In 1534 the islands were ceded to the Portuguese who did nothing with them and in 1661 the major island of the group, Mumbadevi, was given as the wedding dowry of Catherine Braganza to Charles the II of England. Soon after, the British took possession of all seven islands and in 1668 leased them to the East India Company for an annual rent of £10 in gold. But it was only in 1854 after the laying of the railways that the dynamic development of Bombay began.

Most people have a love-hate relationship with Bombay. The extraordinary opulence as well as the poverty seen in Bombay and the human stampede comes as a culture shock not only to the foreign tourist but to the Indians who have grown up in smaller cities. But the tenacious drive and efficiency of its people have won it a coterie of ardent admirers. Art and culture flourish in Bombay, fashions are set and political dramas enacted.

Gateway of India. Opposite the graceful Taj Mahal Hotel, the Gateway of India is an important landmark of Bombay. It was conceived and constructed by a British architect, George Wittet in 1911 to welcome King George the V for the durbar at Delhi. Though it is a conventional arch of triumph, it is made of yellow basalt and is a striking structure around which the people gather to enjoy the cool breeze from the Arabian Sea in the evening. Today it is also the point for launch rides to Elephanta Caves. Close to the Gateway is a statue of Shivaji astride his horse and one of Swami Vivekananda, benign and serene.

Within walking distance of the Gateway are the **Colaba Causeway**; the busy shopping arcade; the **Prince of Wales Museum** with its collection of miniature paintings, images and bas reliefs from the Elephanta Caves and images and models of the Parsee Towers of Silence; **the Jehangir Art Gallery**, the city's principal art gallery; the **University** and **High Court** built in the Gothic style; and **Flora Fountain** which stands in a crowded square in the business heart of Bombay called the Fort area.

Also within walking distance are **Crawford Market** and the **School of Art** where Rudyard Kipling was born and spent his early years. His father, John Lockwood Kipling, designed the bas relief work on Crawford Market. The fort wall from which the area called Fort gets its name has almost disappeared. Only a small fragment survives as part of the boundary wall of St George's Hospital. The finest high Victorian Gothic structure of Bombay is **Victoria Terminus**, popularly known by the abbreviation VT. It is the headquarters of the Central Railway and was constructed between 1878 and 1887. The structure is of yellow sandstone and granite combined with polychromatic stones and blue-gray basalt. But the thousands who rush through the portals every day have no time to admire its grandeur. The other imposing British structures are the Municipal Corporation Building, the Western Railway Central Office at Churchgate, the General Post Office near VT, Ballard Estate and the Afghan Church with its Gothic arches and stained-glass windows.

Mahalakshmi Temple and Racecourse. On the way to the racecourse is the oldest temple of Bombay, the Mahalakshmi Temple dedicated to Lakshmi, the Goddess of Wealth. The idols of the Goddess and her two sisters were found in the sea. The Racecourse is equally famous and takes its name from the temple — the Mahalakshmi Racecourse. Fashion-setters, film stars, gamblers, rich and poor alike converge on these grounds every Sunday from November to March to watch some of the finest horseracing in the country.

Malabar Hill. The drive from Back Bay across Marine Drive to Malabar Hill, the home of Bombay's most affluent, is a good excursion to get the flavor of this cosmopolitan town. At night from the top of the hill you can see the myriad lights of the city twinkling away. The string of glittering lights from Back Bay to Malabar is called the "Queen's Necklace". Poems have been written on the spectacular view of Marine Drive. Late at night when the cars and buses of the city have parked for

the night, the horse-drawn carriages called "Victorias" come out and give rides which add to the magic and romance of Bombay.

On top of Malabar Hill are two famous gardens, the **Hanging Gardens**, with its hedges trimmed to the shape of different animals and across it, the **Kamla Nehru Park**, which is extremely popular with children because it contains an enormous replica of the Old Lady's Shoe from the well-known nursery rhymes.

Chowpatty Beach. Just before Marine Drive swings upwards is the famous Chowpatty Beach of Bombay. Once the scene of political dramas and speech-making, today it is the scene of "good eating". Hundreds of handcarts selling Bombay's delicious *bhel puri* and ice creams dot every inch of the sands and the city pours out to taste their wares. Chowpatty Beach makes the world's best *pau bhajis*, a delicious stuffing of mixed vegetables fried in butter in two pieces of fried buns. Like the India Gate of Delhi, Chowpatty and Marine Drive serve as the green lungs of Bombay.

Elephanta Caves. Bombay is comparatively young and has no monuments of ancient or medieval period. Nine kilometers from the Gateway of India on the Elephanta Island known as Gharapuri (Fortress City), however, are seventh-century rock-cut cave temples dedicated to Lord Shiva. The sculpture of Maheshmurti in the main cave is one of the most renowned pieces of art. In a single carving Shiva is shown as Creator, Protector and Destroyer of the Universe. The massive sculptured panels are chiselled out of the rock walls of the caves and each composition is set in a separate alcove. The other deities of the Hindu pantheon — Brahma and Vishnu — are also shown in the panels. A good, inexpensive ferry service gets you there and back.

Kanheri Caves. About 42 kilometers from Bombay are the 100 Buddhist caves excavated from a huge, circular rock. This is the largest group of Buddhist caves in western India and depict the Hinayana phase of Buddhist architecture. Most of the simpler, smaller caves were used by monks for worship. But the first three caves are more ornate with massive pillars, sculptures and stupas. To reach the Kanheri caves you can take the suburban train to Borivli and then take a bus or taxi.

Juhu, Madh, Marve and Manori beaches are some of the popular beaches of Bombay. While Juhu, just over 20 kilometers from the city proper is crowded, the others, another 20 kilometers further, are comparatively quiet beaches.

Upcountry

GOA. Surrounded by aquamarine blue waters and golden sands this verdant country lies between the Western Ghats and the Arabian Sea, halfway down the west coast.

For 351 years, till 1961, Goa was ruled by the Portuguese. Alfonso de Albuquerque came to India looking for spices, set eyes on this bit of paradise, wrested it from Adil Shah, the Sultan of Bijapur, and stayed on as conquerer.

Despite the many years of foreign domination, it is still very much a part of India today with its healthy integration of cultures and traditions. Elegant, Spanish-style villas, bars that serve *feni*, brewed from cashew and coconut, and the enchanting Goan love songs give Goa a special character that do not detract from its Indianness. Hemmed in by seven of the finest beaches of the world, Goa is fast becoming the Mecca of tourism.

Most of Goa's larger towns are situated in a coastal belt where the Portuguese first settled. Panaji, the capital of Goa, is situated on the southern bank of the Mandovi River and like other towns it is centered on a church and the square in front of it. The **Church of Immaculate Conception** is both an important as well as ancient church of Goa. Built in 1541 its tall twin towers soar above their surrounding areas and for sailors returning home from the long voyages to Lisbon symbolized home. The Municipal Gardens and the Mahalakshmi Temple are the other attractions of the city. But most enjoyable is a walk down the streets of the old residential areas. Here narrow cobbled alleys and tiled roof houses nudging each other with their overhanging balconies and carved columns reflect the Portuguese influence. Interspersed between shops are tiny cafes where the locals tarry for a drink or two to catch up on gossip. After lunch the whole town slumbers for an hour or two.

Beyond the palace square is the pier where the steamers from Bombay dock with an unending number of tourists. Most people coming to Goa from Bombay prefer to come by the steamers which comes most days of the week except in the monsoon months from June to September. The ride, slow and relaxed, prepares you for the ambience of Goa.

The pace in Goa is leisurely and you can walk through the countryside with the gentle strains of the guitar and mandolin pursuing you.

OLD GOA. If Panaji is the administrative capital of Goa, Old Goa is its splendid past. Even before

the Portuguese arrived, it was the second capital of the Adil Shahi dynasty. Unfortunately none of the structures of that period remain except a bit of the gateway to the palace. But the Portuguese nurtured the growth of the city as though it was an extension of Lisbon. Old Goa continued to be the administrative capital of Portugal's eastern empire till 1843 when it was shifted to Panaji. Today it is a small village surrounded by churches and convents, some in active use while others have become museums.

Sé or the **Cathedral of St Catherine** is Old Goa's largest cathedral. Founded by Albuquerque in 1511, it is still used for public service today. A fine example of Renaissance architecture, the cathedral was rebuilt in 1776.

The Convent and Church of St Francis of Assisi with its splendid carvings and old murals depicting the life of Saint Francis was set up by eight priests who arrived there in 1517. Later the chapel put up by them was pulled down and the present building constructed at the spot. The convent at the back of the church has now been converted into an archeological museum.

But it is the **Basilica of Bom Jesus** which is the biggest attraction for Christians. St Francis Xavier who was given the task of spreading Christianity in the east among Portuguese subjects is entombed here almost 150 years after his death. The interior of the church is simple but for the gilded altars, the Italian sculpted tomb of St Francis and the silver casket in which the body of St Francis is displayed.

The other church worth a visit is the **Church of St Cajetan,** modeled on the lines of St Peter's Church in Rome.It was constructed by Italian friars who were sent by the Pope to preach Christianity in Golconda or modern Hyderabad.Since permission was not given by the local authorities the priests settled in Goa.

Churches and beaches are the two basic attractions of Goa. The golden expanse of the beaches dotted with coconut and palm trees are undoubtedly among the best in the world. The problem is more in selecting a good beach from among the profusion available. **Calangute** was the queen of Goa's beaches in the sixties but it has been overexploited. **Baga**, a little further north is excellent. At any time you will find thousands of pilgrims at **Anjuna** or **Chapora** beach. But it is **Colva** beach adjacent to Margao that is considered a bit of paradise. It has 40 kilometers of white, uninterrupted beaches and the sea is blue and calm.

The other attractions of Goa are the **Bondla Wildlife Sanctuary** where you can see sambar and wild boar and the Hindu temples between Panaji and Margao which have survived the demolitions that most temples and mosques were subjected to when the Portuguese arrived.

Goa is well-connected by air, road, rail and sea. There are daily flights too from Bombay but in the tourist season it is necessary to book well in advance. The steamer service to and from Bombay is excellent but stops during the monsoon months. There are several private luxury buses that run to and from Bombay, Bangalore and Belgaum, the latter two being in Karnataka. The railhead in Goa is at Vasco da Gama and you can reach there by ferry to catch a train to Delhi, Bombay and Bangalore. But the journey by train is rather long and tedious especially if you are traveling to Delhi which is almost 47 hours away. Even Bombay and Bangalore are a good 23 to 25 hours from Goa.

AURANGABAD, AJANTA & ELLORA. From Bombay it is also possible to do a four to five days trip to the exquisite ancient **caves of Ajanta and Ellora** near Aurangabad. The antiquity of these caves and paintings has been placed between the 2nd and the 8th century BC.

The Ajanta paintings recount the tales of Lord Buddha and his previous earthly experiences. The opulence of that age comes through in the spacious palace halls, the bejeweled princesses and princes with their retinue of attendants, musicians and market places. The paintings depict celestial musicians and fur-capped foreign emissaries.

Although the theme is primarily religious, the paintings in their range and treatment depict an epic of life during a span of a thousand years. The whole era comes alive in vibrant colors. There is almost a three-dimensional artistry about the paintings and sculptures.

The caves were discovered quite by accident about 150 years ago when a British officer hunting for tigers in the jungles near Aurangabad noticed a glitter in the foliage and rubble. With the help of villagers he discovered the beautifully adorned caves that had become the home of the tigers.

The wall paintings, sculpture and architecture of Ajanta and Ellora are celebrated as a wonder of the ancient world.

The 30 rock-hewn caves at Ajanta, cut into the scarp of a hill, are either Chaityas (chapels) or Viharas (monasteries). Most of them are carved in a manner that allows a flood of natural light to pour into them at any given time.

The most remarkable of the carved shrines at Ellora is the **Kailasa Temple** — 50 meters long, 33 meters wide and 30 meters high. This exquisite temple has been carved by hand from a single rock with gateway, pavilion, courtyard, vestibule, sanctum and tower. The temple is twice the area of the Parthenon and one and a half times as high. It is lavishly carved with epic themes.

Aurangabad is full of historic sites. Apart from the famous caves of Ajanta and Ellora it is possible to see the **Bibika-Maqbara**, the tomb of the wife of Mughal emperor Aurangzeb modeled on the Taj Mahal at Agra, and **Panchakki**, a 17th-century water mill which commemorates a saint.

Some 56 kilometers south of Aurangabad is **Paithan,** famous for its Himroo cotton brocade, woven in gold and silver thread on silk. The motifs are often inspired from the Ajanta paintings.

Aurangabad is connected to Bombay by air, rail and road and about four days should be allotted for a trip to Aurangabad and back.

UDAIPUR is described as a "cool oasis in the dry heart of Rajasthan". Two of its many palaces should not be missed — the Lake Palace which is a hotel and the City Palace which is a museum. The Lake Palace is luxurious and romantic and sits right in the center of a lake. The city has several gardens, fountains, museums and temples. Pichola Lake and Jagdish Temple in the old town with a magnificent bronze statue of Garuda should be on your itinerary. Udaipur is on the airline network that connects it with the major cities of India like Delhi, Bombay and Jaipur.

CHITTORGARH brings alive the legendary romance and chivalry of the Rajputs of a bygone era. It was the first capital of Mewar in the early 13th century. The fort which some say was originally constructed by Bhim, a Pandava prince of Mahabharata fame, was impregnable. A winding one-kilometer long road leads through seven gates to the main gate of the fort.

Chittor was first attacked by Alaud-din Khilji, the Delhi Sultan in 1303. When the fort fell, the women chose to commit *jauhar* (mass self-immolation) rather than be captured.

Two centuries later when it was again with the Rajputs, the Sultan of Gujarat attacked the citadel and when defeat could not be avoided, 13,000 Rajput women committed *jauhar*.

The last and final attack on Chittorgarh took place in 1568 when Mughal emperor Akbar invaded the town. While 8,000 saffron-robed men rode out to battle and death their women immolated themselves.

Today the fort is deserted but there are hundreds of stories and romances etched in stone. The Palace of Rana Kumbha, the Tower of Victory, the Gaumukh Reservoir and Padmini's Palace are just remains of the splendor they once were.

Chittorgarh is 115 kilometers from Udaipur and connected by bus.

KHAJURAHO. Though Khajuraho in Madhya Pradesh, 412 kilometers from Agra and about 200 kilometers from Jhansi, is in a wilderness and not really en route to anywhere or from anywhere, you should not miss the beautiful, ornate temples built by the Chandelas in the 10th and 11th centuries. The temples have survived precisely because of their isolation at a site where there is neither a town or an industry. The Chandelas ruled for five centuries and the 85 Khajuraho temples of which only 22 have survived were the outpourings of their creative genius over a hundred-year period.

The temples were constructed from 950 AD to 1050 AD and are in three distinct groups. Near the newly developed Khajuraho is the western group of temples. In this group can be found the most important of the temples. The eastern group of temples are in and around the old village of Khajuraho. Further to the south are two groups of the southern temples.

These temples have been designed and carved to lead the eyes from ground levels upwards till you seem to be looking at heaven. The world at large identifies the Khajuraho temples with sensual, erotic sculptures. But they are more than just that. The carvings are exquisite and depict the everyday life of the people and the court in that period.

A good time to visit Khajuraho is in March when India's leading dancers perform on the podium of the Khandariya Mahadev Temple. The temples come alive during the dance festival and it seems as if the carved *murtis* have stepped out of the stones to re-enact the pageantry of yesteryears.

There is no railway station at Khajuraho but there is a daily flight from Bombay to Khajuraho by Vayudoot, a feeder airline to the Indian Airlines. Indian Airlines itself also has a daily flight to Khajuraho operating via Delhi-Agra-Khajuraho-Varanasi-Kathmandu. There are also buses daily from Agra, Gwalior and Jhansi to Khajuraho.

Khajuraho has good boarding and lodging facilities. Apart from the temples there is nothing else to see in this township but the temples must not be missed!

The Eastern Region

CALCUTTA. It's overcrowded, it's a commuter's nightmare and it is not the cleanest city, yet a visit to Calcutta is a must because most people say it is the only city with a "soul"!

Calcutta owes its existence to Job Charnok who, in 1686, as chief of the East India Company's factory in Hooghly, selected three adjacent villages — Kalikata, Govindapur and Sutanuti — for their new factory. In 1773, Calcutta became the headquarter of the British administration. Population grew from a few hundred to nearly 100,000 as Calcutta grew in importance. And it hasn't stopped growing. Once with the partition of the subcontinent and again with the creation of Bangladesh — the population swelled again and again to make Calcutta the largest city in India and the fourth largest in the world. Despite all its seemingly insurmountable problems, Calcutta is a city full of life. Music, theater, dance, political rallies, religious celebration — there is never a dull moment in "Cal" as it is popularly called. In Calcutta itself see:

Fort William. This building, on the western extremity of the Maidan was begun in 1757 and took 25 years to complete. It was considered to be amongst the finest forts in the world and is full of familiar history. Kitchener's Mess within the fort was occupied by Lord Kitchener of Khartoum fame when he was Commander-in-Chief in India. Old cannons can be found strategically placed all over Fort William.

The Ochterlony Monument. Situated off Chowringhee, facing the Maidan, the biggest green lung of the city, this monument is a 48-meter column erected to celebrate David Ochterlon's victories in Nepal. It has now been named Shaheed Minar in memory of many freedom fighters.

Chowringhee. Once a jungle path, today it is the city's most elegant shopping-cum-commercial area. Just off Chowringhee is New Market, a shopper's paradise where everything is available under one roof. Bargaining is advised in smaller shops.

Raj Bhavan. The residence of the present governor and erstwhile governor-generals it was built in 1803 by Wellesley. It takes as its model Kedleston Hall in Derbyshire where Lord Curzon was born.

The Writers Building. The seat of the present CPI-M government was built in the late 19th century. The first Writers Building housed the writers of the East India Company, hence the name.

Old China Bazaar. Full of atmosphere it now has no Chinese shops but there is a Parsee fire temple, a mosque and a beautiful Jain temple. It also has two old synagogues, the older of which was built in 1884.

Jorasanko. The stately home of the first family of West Bengal in general and Calcutta in particular, on Sir Hariram Goenka Street, is alive with memories. Every part of the house, every artifact lives and breathes Tagore, India's literary Nobel laureate. Well worth a visit for those interested in literature, art and architecture.

The Botanical Gardens. The Gardens in Howrah were set up in 1786 and has some rare and valuable shrubs and trees. Its pride had been an enormous bayan tree, tthe largest in the world but in 1919 lightning struck the main central trunk. That has been removed but the 1,500 or so offshoots form a circle whose diameter is more than 12 meters.

The Howrah Bridge. The bridge was built in 1941 and every visitor to Calcutta must visit it to get an idea of the mind-boggling 8-lane traffic. Trucks, buses, horse-drawn carriages, buffaloes, bullock carts, sheep and goats form part of the mad scramble to get across from one side to the other. Sometimes when there is a train to catch and traffic has come to a standstill, people just picked up their luggage and run across! On hot days, the bridge increases by 2.5 centimeters in length.

Kalighat Temple. Visit it if you have the stomach for crowds and animal sacrifices. The temple dedicated to Kali was built in 1809 but even before that dacoits (thugs) used to come and pray for success in their mission.

The Victoria Memorial. It houses as its name implies Victorian memorabilia but it also has valuable documents and objects related to the history of West Bengal. It is made entirely of white marble brought all the way from Rajasthan and was inaugurated by the Prince of Wales (later Edward VIII) in 1921. The lawns of the Victoria Memorial are a meeting ground for picnickers, lovers, matchmakers and even film-makers!

Upcountry

DARJEELING. One of the most picturesque of hill stations, Darjeeling is a three-hour drive from Bagdogra Airport up a steep, winding road. It can also be reached by the meter gauge Toy Train from New Jalpaiguri Railway Station. Terrorist activities had discouraged tourism in the last two years but now the little hill station is back to normal and humming with activity. A visit to Darjeeling or Kalimpong, the other hill station a

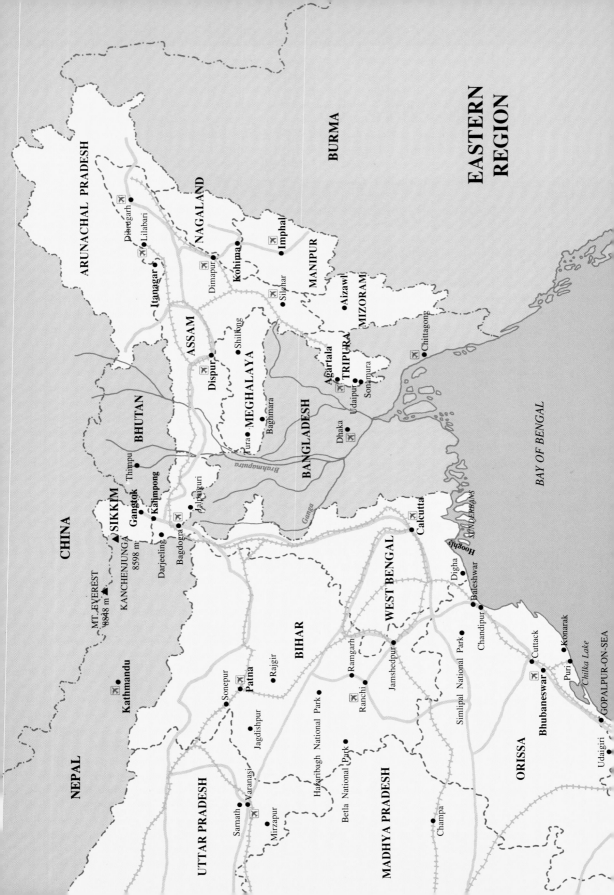

EASTERN
REGION

CHINA

NEPAL

MT. EVEREST
8848 m ▲

KANCHENJUNGA
8598 m ▲

Kathmandu

SIKKIM

Thimpu

BHUTAN

Gangtok
Kalimpong
Darjeeling
Bagdogra
Jalpaiguri

ARUNACHAL PRADESH

Dibrugarh
Lilabari
Itanagar

NAGALAND

Dimapur
Kohima

ASSAM

Dispur
Shillong

MEGHALAYA

Tura
Baghmara

Brahmaputra

Ganga

BANGLADESH

Dhaka

MANIPUR

Imphal

Silchar

MIZORAM

Aizawl

TRIPURA

Agartala
Udaipur
Sonamura

Chittagong

BURMA

UTTAR PRADESH

Sarnath
Varanasi
Mirzapur

BIHAR

Sonepur
Patna
Rajgir

Jagdishpur

Hazaribagh National Park

Betla National Park

MADHYA PRADESH

Champa

Ranchi

Ramgarh

Jamshedpur

WEST BENGAL

Calcutta

Hooghly

SUNDERBANS

Digha

Baleshwar

Chandipur

Simlipal National Park

ORISSA

Bhubaneswar

Cuttack

Puri

Konarak

Chilka Lake

GOPALPUR-ON-SEA

Udaigiri

BAY OF BENGAL

little lower down, needs special permits.

BHUBANESWAR. Bhubaneswar, the capital of Orissa, is 469 kilometers by rail from Calcutta and is known as the city of a thousand temples. The temple architecture is intricately carved and highly decorative and all temples follow the same plan: an inner sanctum sanctorum for the deity, one of several front porches, a dancing hall and a hall of offering. The landscape of Bhubaneswar is dotted with temples that date back to 12th century AD. Behind enormous rocks or standing solitary on an open plain, most of these temples have fallen into disuse yet they are still breathtakingly beautiful. Even twenty years ago you could just walk into a temple compound and pick up an intricately carved piece of sculpture but today all these monuments are protected by the Archeological Survey of India.

The Lingaraj Temple. Built in 1114 AD this temple of Bhubaneswar is dedicated to Shiva. Within the large temple complex are smaller temples dedicated to various gods and goddesses. The entire temple is covered with sculptures, some of them erotic. Non-Hindus are not permitted. Other temples to visit are Vaital Deul, Parasurameswara, Mukteswara and Rajrani.

Udaigiri and Khandagiri Caves. Five kilometers from Bhubaneswar they are the remnants of Buddhist and Jain influences in Orissa. Situated on two hills on either side of the road, these caves were originally used by Buddhist monks. Some of the caves are sculpted and one of the caves, Hathi Gumpha, has an inscription that tells of the exploits of its builder, King Kharavela of Kalinga who ruled from 168-153 BC. If you want peace and quiet, just spend a half day wandering about these caves.

Dhaulagiri. On a hill eight kilometers from Bhubaneswar are the edicts of Ashoka engraved on either side of a sculpted elephant. The hill overlooks the battlefield of Kalinga where Ashoka, horrified by the needless slaughter is said to have laid down arms and embraced Buddhism.

PURI. Puri, 60 kilometers from Bhubaneswar, is the home of the great Jagannath, known in the west as Juggernaut. It is one of the biggest pilgrimmage places in India. Devotees throng the temple, particularly when the great Rath Yatra takes place. Every year in June-July the deities Jagannath, Balaram and Subhadra are placed in enormous, heavy ceremonial chariot 13 meters high, and wheeled from the temple to Mandir 1.5 kilometers away and back again after seven days — symbolic of the gods going home and return-

ing. People jostle and push to have a glimpse of the deity and also to pull the heavy chariot for a short distance. It is said whoever does so is ensured of a place in heaven and many deliberately throw themselves under the heavy wheels and commit suicide for it is believed that death under Jagannath's wheels gets them *moksha* or *nirvana*, that is, deliverance from rebirths. All temples run kitchens where food is made as offerings for the gods. This is called *prasad* and is later distributed free or sold for a small fee to the pilgrims. The kitchens of the Jagannath temple are the largest of all temple kitchens.

Puri has one of the loveliest beaches in the country — the sea is a clear blue and the surf is inviting but it can get rough sometimes, so it is best to take along a *nulia* or one of the local lifeguards who are superb swimmers. The little urchins that hang about the beach are also excellent swimmers. Drop a coin into the sea and watch them fish it out for you!

KONARAK. The Sun Temple in Konarak, some 65 kilometers from Bhubaneswar, is known the world over for its exquisite carvings. Built in the shape of a chariot with 12 pairs of wheels of eight spokes each, it is drawn by seven horses. One of the original horses is missing.

The first sun temple was built in this place in the 9th century but when it fell into decay, the present one was built in the 13th century. It took 1,200 artisans 16 years to build. The temple had a 70-meter high *deul* or sanctum sanctorum and a 40-meter high *Jaganmohan* or outer portico but the *deul* collapsed in the middle of the 19th century. When it was built the sea touched its shores but today it is some three kilometers away. Yet a visit to the seashore is not to be missed. The seashore is wild and lovely and the sea washes up some of the most beautiful shells.

The best time to visit Konarak is in the early morning. As the sun rises, the first rays touch the innermost part of the sanctum sanctorum — such was the engineering genius of the builders!

CHILKA LAKE. South of Bhubaneswar is Chilka Lake, India's largest saltwater lake. Many migratory birds use it as a stopover from December to January. There are buses daily connecting Puri with Calcutta, Bhubaneswar and Konarak.

GOPALPUR-ON-SEA. A seaside resort, it is 95 kilometers from Bhubaneswar. It is quieter than Puri but for nature lovers it is ideal. If you are lucky, you can watch Ridley turtles beach and lay eggs in August.

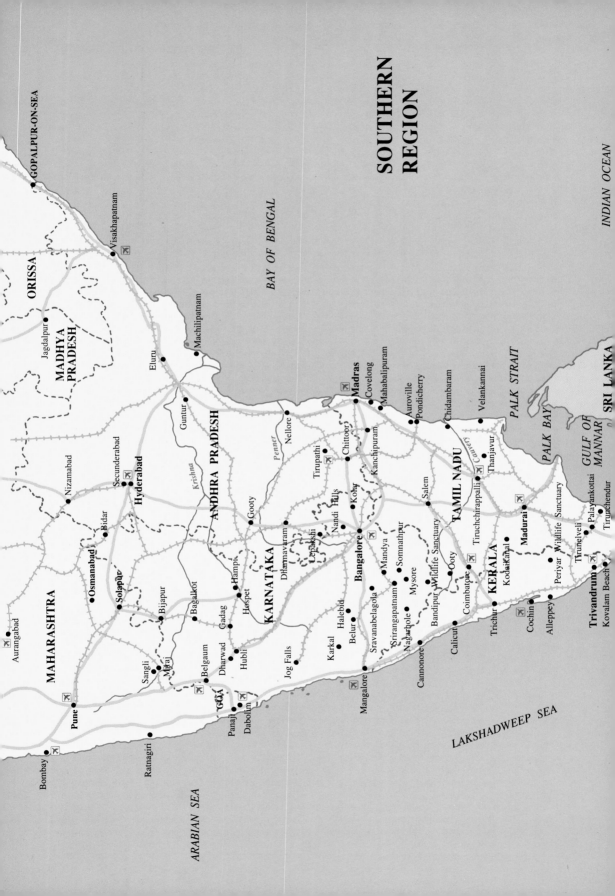

SOUTHERN
REGION

INDIAN OCEAN

ORISSA

GOPALPUR-ON-SEA

Visakhapatnam

BAY OF BENGAL

MADHYA
PRADESH

Jagdalpur

SRI LANKA

Machilipatnam

Eluru

Madras
Covelong
Mahabalipuram
Auroville
Pondicherry
Chidambaram
Velankannai

PALK STRAIT

Nizamabad

Secunderabad
Hyderabad

ANDHRA PRADESH

Guntur

Nellore

Tirupathi

Chittoor
Kolar
Kanchipuram

Salem

Thanjavur

PALK BAY
GULF OF
MANNAR

Krishna

Penner

Gooty

Bidar

Osmanabad

Solapur

Bijapur

Bagalkot

Hampi

Dharwavaram

Lepakshi

Nandi Hills

Bangalore

Mandya
Somnathpur

TAMIL NADU

Cauvery

Tiruchchirappalli

Madurai

Palayankottai
Tirunelveli
Tirunchendur

MAHARASHTRA

Aurangabad

Gadag

Hospet

KARNATAKA

Mysore

Ooty

Bandipur Wildlife Sanctuary

KERALA

Periyar Wildlife Sanctuary

Kodaikanal

Sangli
Miraj

Belgaum
Dharwad
Hubli

Karkal

Halebid
Belur

Sravanabelagola
Srirangapatnam

Nagarhole

Coimbatore

Trichur

Trivandrum

Kovalam Beach

Panaji
Dabolim

GOA

Jog Falls

Cannonore

Calicut

Cochin
Alleppey

Bombay

Ratnagiri

Mangalore

ARABIAN SEA

LAKSHADWEEP SEA

Pune

The Southern Region

MADRAS. The capital of Tamil Nadu, the gateway to south India and the fourth largest city of India after Delhi, Bombay and Calcutta, Madras is a center for culture, rich in its vibrant traditions of music, dance and crafts that have retained their pristine purity.

It's the land of Bharat Natyam, the most popular classical Indian dance today. The music is that of the saint-poet Thyagaraja and recalls the legendary musicians and prized sculptures in stone and bronze. The 61 centimeters high bronze statue of Nataraja-Shiva in the cosmic dance pose that has become symbolic of Indian art can be seen at the Madras National Art Gallery. At the Kalakshetra School at Adayar the dance traditions of the south are still fervently taught and practiced, other arts encouraged and the ancient designs of Indian textiles are adapted for modern use and markets.

The people, their language, the way they think, look and dress is radically different from people in north India. It is the land of the dark-skinned, ebony-haired Dravidians. The Tamilian names are tongue twisters and reflect their professions or ancestral villages. But most of them have been abbreviated for convenience.

The men wear dhotis, lengths of starched white cotton with gold or black lines on the border for embellishment. Wrapped around the lower part of the body like a sarong, the dhoti is ideal for the intense heat of the south. The women who wear exquisite silk saris, often tucked between the legs, love jewelry (particularly diamonds) and their long, lustrous hair is invariably adorned with flowers. The foreheads of the religious Tamils are often adorned with caste signs in sandalwood paste or vermillion and ashes.

The 5,000 year old civilization of the south has remained untouched by the foreign invaders who virtually shaped the destinies of the people north of the Vindhya Mountains. The Pallavas, the Cholas and Pandyas gave Tamil Naidu its architectural and cultural heritage. The Europeans reached the deep south only 350 years ago. But they too left their stamp.

Though the Europeans first settled in Madras before branching out into other cities, it is the least westernized of the four big cities of India. In AD 78 "doubting Thomas" or Thomas the Apostle came to India as a missionary and was martyred on St Thomas Mount, near what is now Madras Airport. A residential area of Madras and a cathedral have been named San Thome after him.

But the history of Madras really began with the arrival of the British in 1639. The Raja of Chandragiri is said to have given Francis Day a lease to open a trading post of the British East India Company on the site of Madras known as Madraspatram. The Fort St George, from which the British held Madras till India achieved independence, was constructed by 1653.

Fort St George. The fascinating story of early British history in India was very often enacted from this historic fort. It was here that Lord Clive came as a clerk of the Company in 1743. When the fort was captured by the French, Clive escaped and came back as an officer in the army of the East India Company.

Modern Madras has grown around this fortress and its six-meter high wall which still stands sturdy today. The house of Clive and Lord Wellesley, who later became the Duke of Wellington, are still intact. India's oldest Anglican church is also inside the fort. In the church is a register in which Clive's marriage is entered. Clive is also buried in the church's graveyard. Georgetown, the original Madras, lies to the north of the fort.

The Marina. The most prominent feature of Madras is its beach, the second biggest in the world, which runs from the harbor in the north to the cathedral in the south. The waters of the sea are a clean, deep blue unlike the grey of the Arabian Sea in the west. Swimming is discouraged in the shark-infested seawaters of Madras but there is nothing to stop sunbathing on the beaches.

The City. The city can be divided into two parts. The older section is west of the dock area and north of Poonamallee High Road. A lot of offices and local markets are situated here adding to the congestion. At Parry's Corner, a well-known landmark of the area, there is a good flower and fruit market. But it is the Burma Bazaar, a collection of 500 shops opposite the bus stop, with its assortment of electronic goods and other merchandise, that is a big attraction. Shopping can be fun here, especially if you are the kind that likes bargain. Slums, which are a depressing feature of every big city of India, have come up in the heart of the city area.

The modern part of the city commences south of Poonamallee Road from Fort St George. On Anna Salai Road, popularly known as Mount Road, are the tourist and airlines offices, banks, important shopping and business centers. Just off Mount Road are the deluxe hotels.

Film Industry. If Bombay is the Hollywood of India, Madras is the throbbing heart of south India

film industry. The city has innumerable film production studios and a large number of its politicians, particularly the chief ministers, have moved from the celluloid screen to the political arena. The south Indian film heroines are well rounded and buxom and the heroes oily haired and not exactly handsome. But they have a tremendous following and garish billboards all over the city keep the people posted about the unending stream of film extravaganzas.

Temples and Shrines. To get the flavor of the south you must visit the temples for their artistic, architectural allure as well as to get a feel of the intense piety of the people. In the old city of Mylapore is the Kapaliswarar Temple, dedicated to Lord Kapaliswarar or Shiva. The *gopuram* or the top part of the temple has been destroyed or severed but this has not detracted from the beauty of the temple or its religious significance. A festival is held every year to commemorate the miracle performed by a Shaivite saint (a disciple of Shiva) in resurrecting a dead girl.

Parthasarthi Shrine, dedicated to Lord Vishnu in the Triplicane area of the city, was built by the early Pallava rulers in the 8th century and has some interesting carvings.

National Art Gallery and Museum. In the Victorian Gothic building on Pantheon Road is housed the National Art Gallery. Next to it is the government museum with some exciting bronzes, sculptures and architectural pieces of the Dravidian rulers.

Guindy Snake Park. No visit to Madras is complete without a visit to Guindy and its Snake Park and Conservation Center. Founded by Romulus Whittaker, an American settled in India, it has over 500 snakes, housed in open pits where they can be seen moving and feeding in their natural environs. In a country which venerated and worships snakes, the Whitakers seek to demystify them by allowing the public to touch, feel and photograph them. Also on show are crocodiles, alligators, monitor lizards and chameleons.

Upcountry

A visit to Madras is incomplete unless you see Mahabalipuram and Kanchipuram, 58 and 76 kilometers south and southwest of Madras respectively, reflecting the glory and greatness of the Pallava emperors.

MAHABALIPURAM was the main harbor and naval base of the Pallava empire in the 7th century AD. But today the thriving port of the Pallavas is

a sleepy village living on its past glory and the tourist traffic. The Pallavas built some exquisite monuments, the best known being the Shore Temple. The sculptures and stone carvings are fascinating.

Mahabalipuram is also known as the "city of the seven pagodas" for out of solid stone were carved exquisite rock temples. Five of the temples are known as "rathas" or chariots and on their walls the story of Hindu mythology has been lovingly carved out. Small and well-proportioned the temples are no more than 10.5 to 13.7 meters high.

The most famous of them is a group of five *rathas*, the chariots on which the princes of yore went out to battle. This *ratha* is dedicated to the five Pandava princes and their consort-wife, Draupadi. Life-size statutes of an elephant, a lion and bull seem to be guarding the temple.

A fresco in stone that has so much vitality and vibrance that it seems to be alive is the "penance of Bhagiratha". This is said to be the world's largest bas-relief and a masterpiece in composition — some 25 meters long and 6 meters high. A group of elephants, one of them 5 meters long, known as "Arjuna's Penance" is the most prominent feature of this sculpture.

Though most of the rock temples have been affected by the ingress of the salt-laden seawaters, the Shore Temple, built by King Rajasimha in the 7th century and dedicated to Lord Vishnu has been protected against erosion. This is a tall, graceful temple with the blue waters of the sea as its backdrop. Alongside the main temple are smaller pyramid-like structures crowned by similar octagonal domes. A row of magnificently carved bulls surround the temple. Mahabalipuram too has a fine beach with several resort facilities.

KANCHIPURAM, the golden city, is about 65 kilometers west of Mahabalipuram. This was the capital of the Pallavas and the city of a thousand temples of which 124 have withstood the ravages of time.

En route to Kanchipuram you can stop at Thirukalikunram, eight kilometers west of Mahabalipuram, where every day just before noon, the priest of the temple, situated on a 152-meter hill, feeds two white kites said to be the spirits of saints. That is why this place of pilgrimage is also known as Pakshithirtham or "Bird Pilgrimage". At the foot of the hill is another rock temple dedicated to Shiva.

Kanchipuram is the holy city of both Lord Shiva and Lord Vishnu and it is for this reason that

Kanchipuram is one of the seven holy cities of India and on the pilgrim route. The other cities are Hardwar, Ujjain, Varanasi, Mathura, Ayodhya and Dwarka. Some have also called Kanchipuram, the "Varanasi of the south".

Kanchipuram was the capital of the Pallavas, the Cholas and the rulers of Vijayanagaram. Though the temples in this city of Gods and erstwhile kings date back to the 4th century, the finest temples were constructed in the 6th and 7th centuries. Kanchi was also the seat of learning and Hindu and Buddhist philosophies flourished side by side. Today, it is the center of handwoven silks of India. Kanchipuram saris, known as Kanjeevaram, are thick and of excellent quality. No south Indian wedding is complete unless there are a couple of exquisite Kanjeevarams in the bride's trousseau.

But it is the temples that bring the religious and the connoisseurs of temple art to Kanchipuram. The oldest temple, constructed in sandstone by the Pallavas, the Kailasantha Temple, is dedicated to Lord Shiva. On the walls of the tiny cells surrounding its courtyard are some excellent Pallava paintings dating back to the 7th and 8th centuries. These and the paintings in the Vaikunthanatha Perumal Temple built by Nandi Varman II are said to be among the finest Hindu murals of that era. The sculptures here relate to wars fought by the Pallavas and Chalyukas.

Equivalent to the dreaming spires of Oxford are the *gopurams* or the temple tops of the later temples of Kanchipuram. Minutely carved they have given a special character to the city. The Ekambareswara Temple stands 57 meters tall and has no less than 10 stories of intricate carvings.

The Varadarajaswamy Vishnu Temple is smaller but even it has a tower 30.5 meters tall. A main hall with 96 ornately sculpted pillars is the temple's special feature. In the courtyard of the temple is an ancient mango tree, the four branches of which, according to legend, represent the four Vedas. The fruits from each of the four branches taste different and those who eat them are said to be eternally wise. The two main temple builders of Kanchipuram were Mahendra Varman and Mamalla Narisimha Varman who founded Mahabalipuram. In their regime Kanchipuram became a leading center of arts, architecture and philosophy.

PONDICHERRY. About 150 kilometers south of Madras on the east coast of India lies Pondicherry, a former French town and now one of India's union territories. It is so different from the rest of south India and so much like a sleepy French village that a visit is worthwhile especially for those seeking a tranquil holiday. It was only in 1954, seven years after Indian independence and after 250 years of French rule that Pondicherry was returned to India.

The French developed the town into an important trading center. The heart of the city today contains the Raj Nivas, the official residence of the Lieutenant Governor and other government buildings. A statue of Dupleix who governed Pondicherry for 40 years still stands near the government house by the sea.

In the old French area the streets are cobbled as in a French town. The policemen still wear very French kepis and a statue of Joan of Arc completes the French setting.

Ten kilometers from the town is the Hindu ashram of Sri Aurobindo and the new city of Auroville. Sri Aurobindo who played an active role in India's freedom struggle was an important religious philosopher who believed that human beings should live close to nature in complete harmony with their fellow beings. The ashram, its orchards and colleges attract a large number of foreigners and it looks like a mini United Nations. The atmosphere at Pondicherry has been described as "Sachidananda" or pure of spirit.

CHIDAMBARAM. Deeper south, if you can hire a car and travel all the way up to Rameswaram, there are many more famous temple cities. Three to four hours drive from Pondicherry bring you to Chidambaram and the 9th-century Nataraja Temple of Chidambaram. It is here that Nataraja-Shiva is said to have performed his cosmic dance for Parvati and in December when the Betelguse star is on the ascendant a festival is held here and thousands of devotees come for worship. The God at Chidambaram is visualized as "ethereal, all-permeating and soul filling."

The granite temple, spread across 13 hectares of flat land between two rivers and surrounded by a wall 600 meters by 500 meters, is covered with sculptures depicting the 108 stances of the Natya Shastra, the science of dancing. Inside the temple are five courts and in the most striking of these courts, decorated with a thousand pillars, the Pandyas and Cholas who built the temple are said to have held their victory celebrations. The magnificent statue of Nataraja at Chidambaram is cast in an alloy of five metals. Vishnu is also worshiped at the Govindaraja Temple of Chidambaram. The temple is of a later period but the statue

of Lord Vishnu on a bed of snakes is a superb piece of workmanship.

THANJAVUR is the city of the Chola rulers and bears their stamp in an array of temples finely sculpted and carved. The Brihadesvara Temple built by Raja Chola is said to have been the tallest monument in ancient India, rising to a height of 92 meters in pyramidal form. The painted murals of the Cholas in the covered walking area around the sanctum, are in rich color with exquisite details. Near the inner shrine of Brihadesvara is a gigantic, five-meter long black granite sculpture of Nandi, the bull of Lord Shiva.

At Thanjavur you can also visit the Subramanya Temple. The Shivaganga Tank and Schwartz Church were built by an Indian ruler to express his friendship for a Danish missionary.

Close to Thanjavur is Tiruvayur, the home of the saint and composer Sri Thyagaraja. In his honor a major music festival is held here every January.

MADURAI. Undoubtedly the high point of a visit to the temple cities is Madurai. While modern travelers have called it "the beating heart" of Tamil Nadu, historians have associated the sweetness of Madurai, as its name implies, to the nectar that fell from the hair of Lord Shiva.

Legends, myths and the reality of thousands of pilgrims swarming to the city every day have interwoven to give Madurai its unique character and ambience.

The Meenakshi Temple, with its ten towering *gopurams*, raised by the Nayaks who ruled Madurai from the middle of the 16th century to the middle of the 18th century is the focal point of the city and hub of major activity. Whether you come by air, train or road, the first glimpse of the city is of the magnificent *gopurams* of Madurai.

Though it was the Nayaks who built the famous temple, the culture and the love of fine arts in the city can be traced back to the 14th century and the Pandyas whose capital it was. Tamil literature flourished under their patronage in the city but it was the Nayaks who gave the city the magnificent landmark of the Meenakshi Temple.

At Madurai only the believers can enter the sanctuaries where Meenakshi and Shiva in his incarnation of Sundereswara are enshrined. But they have access to all other areas of the temple. You can even climb to the top of one of the *gopurams* and get an excellent view of the city.

All year round, any time of day or night the temple is filled with worshipers. But the greatest day at the temple comes towards the end of April when the wedding of the main deities is re-enacted to the chanting of mantras and the playing of the *nadaswaram* (wind woodhorn). The deities are paraded through the streets and for three days there are festivities.

Elsewhere in the city too the architectural genius of the Nayaks can be seen in the palace of Tirumala Nayak. In the evenings it is the venue for a *son et lumiere* show.

BANGALORE. In 1937, Winston Churchill visited Bangalore. He wrote "We . . . posting in all our resources took a palatial bungalow, all pink and white with a heavy tiled-roof and deep verandahs sustained by white plaster columns weathered in purple bougainvillaea." Much of Bangalore, the capital of Karnataka, is still bougainvillaea and pink roses and no wonder it is called the "Garden City of India".

Bangalore is one of the prettiest cities of India with a salubrious climate, open parks and tree-lined avenues. Situated 1,000 meters above sea-level, it is fast becoming like Dehradun, below Mussoorie in Uttar Pradesh, the home of the old and the retired. Simultaneously there has been a significant growth of the city with several industries coming up including the famous watch and aircraft manufacturing units of the country.

But like other big metropolises, Bangalore had a humble beginning in 1537 when Kempe Gowda, a local chieftain, built a mud fort on a hill. It became an important fortress city under Hyder Ali and Tippu Sultan in the 18th century though there are few remains from this period except for Lal Bagh Botanical Gardens. Today the Kempe Gowda Circle is a busy and important landmark in the city.

When you visit the city of Lal Bagh by car, plan for a six to seven hours tour. The botanical gardens, four kilometers from the city, were laid out by Hyder Ali, the Muslim chieftain who overthrew the Wodeyar dynasty. But it was his son, Tipu Sultan, who developed it into a summer garden. Spread over 97 hectares with a thousand different trees and plants and a central glasshouse where flower shows are held in August and February, it is today one of the best gardens in the country.

Cubbon Park. One of the main lungs of the city, this 121-hectare park was laid out in 1864. Landscaped into it are the red Gothic building of the public library, the High Court, the government museum and the technological and industrial museum. The government museum set up in 1886

has some rare artifacts of geology, art, numismatics and relics from Mohenjodaro, one of the cradles of Indian civilization.

The Vidhan Soudha. A magnificent post-idependence building in granite it houses the secretariat and state legislature. The architecture is neo-Dravidian. The Cabinet room is famous for its massive pure sandalwood door. The building is floodlit on Sunday evenings and public holidays.

The Bull Temple. One of Bangalore's oldest temples is the Bull Temple on Bugle Hill. It was built by Kempe Gowda in the Dravidian style and has a huge monolith of Nandi, the vehicle of Shiva. Non-Hindus are allowed into the temple.

WHITE FIELDS. If you want to see a faith healer and a religious leader with a following of several thousands both in India and abroad, a visit to White Fields, the ashram (religious retreat) of the renowned Satya Sai Baba, 16 kilometers from Bangalore, is called for. With his deep saffron robes and black, crinkly hair spread around his head like a halo, the Sai Baba is an impressive figure. He literally materializes from the air rings, small statuettes of gods and goddesses and *vibhuti* or sacred ash that the sages of India smear over their forehead. People from all over the country rich and poor alike, some with terminal stages of cancer, come to him confident that his touch can cure them.

BANNARGHATTA. 21 kilometers from Bangalore is the safari park of Bannarghatta. With an area of 104 square kilometers it is continuously being developed as a wildlife reserve. A snake park and a crocodile farm have also been developed inside the reserve.

NANDI HILLS. 68 kilometers from Bangalore it is a popular hill station which even in the days of Tippu Sultan was a popular summer retreat. A 600-meter cliff face called Tippu's drop provides a splendid view of the adjoining area.

KOLAR GOLD FIELDS. Located 100 kilometers east of Bangalore the Kolar Fields have the deepest mine shafts in the world, some of them 3,000 meters below the surface. They are the major gold producers for India. A visit to the mines is possible with special permission.

From Bangalore there are one-day tours to Sravanabelagola, Srirangapatnam, Mysore City and the Brindavan Gardens. There are also one-day excursions to Belur and Halebid.

SRAVANABELAGOLA. From Bangalore plan a visit to the magnificent, 17-meter tall statue of Lord Bahubali (Gomatesvara). The statue, the tallest in the world, has been carved out of a single rock. It stands on Indragiri Hill, below which nestles the small town of Sravanabelagola. Today it is an important Jain pilgrim center.

According to legend, Bahubali was the youngest son of a Jain emperor who ruled over a kingdom in north India and later became a Jain saint. When he renounced the world a battle broke out between his two sons for succession. Though Bahubali emerged the victor, in his hour of triumph he realized the futility of worldly success, gave the kingdom to his brother and retired to the forest for penance of a thousand years. The giant sculpture of the naked Bahubali (a sect of the Jain where its religious leaders do not wear clothes) was completed in 981 AD.

Once every 12 to 14 years a religious ritual called "mahamastakabhisheka" is performed at Sravanabelagola and the Lord's head is anointed with thousands of pots of coconut milk, yogurt, ghee, bananas, dates, almonds, silver, honey, gold and sandalwood paste. A special scaffolding is erected for people to reach the head. Thousands of pilgrims from all over India descend on the sleepy township for this ritual. In 1981, a million people witnessed the grand anointment celebrating a thousand years of the erection of the statue.

SRIRANGAPATNAM. On the Bangalore road sixteen kilometers from Mysore stands the ruins of Hyder Ali and Tippu Sultan's famous capital, Srirangapatnam or "Seringapatam" as the British called it. It was from here in the 18th century that Tippu controlled most of southern India till he was defeated by the British. There is not much of the old Srirangapatnam left, for the British did a good job of demolishing it. But the extensive stone walls, gates and the dungeon where Tippu held some British officers as prisoners have been preserved. Inside the walls are a mosque and the Sri Ranganathaswamy Temple, a popular place of pilgrimage for the Hindus.

Across the ruins of the ancient capital is Daria Daulat Bagh, Tippu's summer palace and the Gumbaz, Tippu's mausoleum. The summer palace with their ornate arches and ceilings are famous for their beautiful paintings and galleries. There is an array of paintings depicting his campaigns against the British.

MYSORE. You can almost smell the fragrance before you reach the city. The air is laden with the heady scent of sandalwood, joss-sticks and incense and *mallige* or jasmine. Mysore is also the city of elephants. The elephant is the state symbol

and exquisite woodcarved elephants inlaid with ivory make good souvenirs.

Mysore city till independence was the seat of the Maharajas of Mysore — a princely state covering much of the present-day Karnataka. The ex-ruler who is also a member of Parliament, lives in a part of the grand palace today. The exquisite architecture of the palace in Indo-Saracenic style draws visitors throughout the year. In keeping with the lavish style of those days even ordinary buildings have ornate domes and vaulting archways.

Gone are the days of palace splendor and luxury. Only a glimpse of that magnificence can be had in the 10 days of Dussehra festivity in early October. The erstwhile ruler leads a grand procession of richly caparisoned elephants, liveried retainers, cavalry and images of deities with brass and jazz bands in tow. It's an extravaganza and a treat that one should not miss.

Chamundi Hill. This hill in Mysore provides a challenge to the daily throngs of pilgrims to the Chamundeswari Temple. You have to climb a thousand steps (about four kilometers) to reach the top of the hill and the temple which has a seven-storied high *gopuram*. The climb is strenuous but the view from the top is exhilarating. Even half way up you can get an excellent view of Mysore city and the surrounding countryside. Almost near the top is the five-meter high Nandi (Shiva's bull), carved out of stone. For those not keen on walking there is a motorable road and a good bus and taxi service.

BRINDAVAN GARDENS. 19 kilometers northwest of Mysore these gardens are beautifully laid out with perennial shrubs and water pools. At night the gardens change into an exotic fairyland with myriad-colored fountains and twinkling lights. Brindavan Gardens are also popular with film-makers and you might chance upon a film hero or heroine prancing about the lawns or traipsing among the trees and shrubs.

SOMNATHPUR. Forty-five kilometers east of Mysore is the exquisite Channakeshara Temple of Somnathpur. Built by the Hoysala kings at the height of their power in 1260 AD, the star-shaped temple is covered with superb sculptures depicting scenes from the epics, the *Ramayana* and the *Mahabharata*, and the life and times of the Hoysala people.

BANDIPUR WILDLIFE SANCTUARY. This sanctuary is part of a bigger national park which includes Mudumalai in Tamil Nadu and Wynad in Kerala. Here you can see the majestic Indian elephant roaming freely, often in large herds. If you are lucky, you may catch a glimpse of the Indian bison called "Gaur", the tiger and leopard — all of them elusive creatures. At Mudumalai, elephants take you to the heart of the jungles and sitting in the safety of your motorized boat you can sight crocodiles basking in the sun and animals drinking water at sunset.

BELUR AND HALEBID. The Hoysalas ruled in the Deccan between the 11th and 13th centuries. The temples at Belur and Halebid, which remained incomplete despite 80 years of labor, are their offerings of the finest workmanship in stone to the Gods. The intricately sculptured decorations on the temple, according to some critics are even better than the friezes at Konarak in Orissa and Khajuraho in Madhya Pradesh. Scenes from hunting, agriculture, music and dancing, including some erotic scenes have been carved in the inner and outer walls of the temples.

The temple at Halebid, the capital of the Hoysalas, was started 10 years after the Belur Temple. At Belur, the Channekeshava Temple is the only one of three Hoysala sites which is still used for worship. Here much of the workmanship has gone into the internal supporting pillars.

As with the Mysore Palace the glory has faded into the pages of history. Halebid today is a rural village and Belur a small town, and the temples only a testimony to their past glory.

HAMPI. Located in North Karnataka this is the ruins of what was the capital of the famous Vijayanagar empire in the 14th-15th century. Now on the World Heritage List, the medieval ruins cover some 26 square kilometers interspersed with sugarcane fields and food crops. The Tungabhadra River also zig-zags through this hill country strewn with enormous rounded boulders.

There is a magical quality to the ruins of Hampi even 650 years after the empire of Krishnadevaraya disintegrated. Though only 26 of the original 33 square kilometers of the old empire remain, there is still so much to see that it is not possible to see it in one day on foot.

But you can hire a cycle and zip around avoiding the stray cattle in the area. Don't miss the Vittala Temple with its famous stone chariot and the elaborately carved musical pillars. Or the Purandara Dasara Mandapa (the riverside temple), the Sule and Hampi Bazaars, the Achutaraya Temple, the palace area with its platform, lotus mahal, elephant stables and watchtower, the Hazarama Temple and the Queen's Bath.

Best Bets

ANTIQUES. Bombay is the city for antiques. At Chor Bazaar at the end of Muhammad Ali Road from Saturday to Thursday antiques can be picked up for a song. Chandeliers, Chinese old plates and umpteen other bric-a-brac can be collected. On Friday, the same area is converted into a flea market selling a range of second-hand items ranging from rugs to stereo systems and videos.

At Jogeshwari, about 45 minutes by train from Bombay Central, a new antique market has come up that specializes in rosewood furniture.

Just behind the famous Taj Hotel is a lane with shops selling antiques — statues, bronzes, wood-carvings and vintage glass.

BOMBAY'S THEATER WORLD is the best developed in the country and almost throughout the year there will be some theatrical activity at the Prithvi Theater in Juhu.

English, Hindi as well as Marathi plays are staged here every evening from 7.45 pm. Bombay's top film and stage personalities produce as well as act in the plays staged here and the auditorium is invariably full. Sometimes the plays run for a couple of years as they move from theater to theater. In addition to the Prithvi Theaters, plays are staged at the NTPC, the Nehru Center at Worli, Tejpal Auditorium near August Kranti Maidan and Sophia College off Peddar Road.

MINIATURE INDIA. India is a shopper's paradise. If you don't have the time to shop on your tour of India, you can do so at Delhi at Baba Kharak Singh Marg. Every state of the country has a showroom or shop here. You can pick up cane baskets of Assam, papier mâché boxes of Kashmir, Darjeeling tea and lacquer bangles of Rajasthan. Since the shops are government run, prices are reasonable and you can be sure of the quality of the product purchased. Several shops sell precious and semi-precious stones.

ETHNIC CHIC. For those with a taste for the upmarket, Khazana at Taj Mahal Hotel on Mansingh Road, Delhi, offers a wide and excellent choice of goods to choose from. Though the goods at Khazana are on the pricey side, many of them are also exclusive. Most of the products — whether it is a length of textile or an item of pottery — are ethnic and chic. You can have your pick of products in this treasure house which includes handicrafts, antiques and curios, pottery and miniature paintings, Tanjore plates, leather goods, silks from all parts of the country, costume jewelry and jewelry in gold and precious stones. Tel. 3016162.

FABINDIA is an appropriate name for a fabulous shop! Fabindia, tucked away in the north block market of Greater Kailash I in New Delhi caters to the tourist who is looking for exclusive designs in handloom textiles and fitting ready-made garments. Started in 1960, Fabindia sold textiles with ethnic designs and weaves — curtains, bedcovers and table linen. Ikat, the famous weave of Orissa and Andhra Pradesh is very popular. You can find woollens too — *pattus*, the large carpet-like shawls from Rajasthan, woollen cushion covers and bedspreads.

HERBAL BEAUTY. India has a rich tradition of natural beauty aids. Unlike the many synthetic cosmetics found in the west, the Indian herbal beauty aids are derived from fruits and from the roots of herbs. One person who has raised this traditional knowledge to a fine art is Shahnaz Husain whose creams, soaps, moisturizers and hair conditioners have been such a phenomenal success that the French have signed a contract for import of her cosmetics. For that glowing vibrant look a visit to one of the many Shahnaz beauty parlors should not be missed.

INDIAN PERFUMES. The Indian perfume (*attar*) industry is one of the oldest in the world. Formed of a unique concentrate which has its base in sandalwood oil instead of industrial alcohol it has withstood competition from French perfumes for almost 400 years. You can pick up a bottle of Indian attar from Kanauj and Lucknow in Uttar Pradesh or Khari Baoli in Old Delhi.

DRINKING FENI. No trip to Goa is complete unless you sip *feni*, a local brew made out of the cashew fruit and coconut, at a pub. This should be followed by a Goan meal of pork *vindaloo* and prawn curry. Though Goan chefs, prawn curry and their swinging bands can now be found at major hotels in India, the best music and food is still in Goa itself. Maybe there is something to be said for the setting.

DELHI WEDDINGS. In India, weddings are not private affairs, so if you are in Delhi invite yourself to a Delhi wedding. It is an extravaganza with colorful lights and fireworks. The groom comes riding on a white mare, his face covered with strings of marigolds and jasmines and a garland of rupee notes round his neck. There may be anything from 500 to 1000 guests — a lot of them gatecrashers — and each of them is welcomed by the sprinkling of rose essence.

INDIAN TEA. India's Darjeeling tea, with its natural bouquet, is considered the world's finest. It is best drunk without milk or just a wee drop. Down

south in India, the Blue Mountains (Nilgiri Hills) produce special teas with a distinct character. You could drink it with a teaspoon of milk as the leisurely tea-planter does, to enjoy nature in his cup. The thick gutty tea of Assam has no parallel. Traditionally known as the English Breakfast cup it comes from the densely forested areas of northeast India. This tea tastes best with plenty of milk up to 30 milliliters per cup. Make sure you buy the best to enjoy its tropical green character.

WEAVERS BAZAAR. If you want to pick up an exquisitely woven Indian sari from the famous looms of Varanasi, take time off to visit the "satti" or weavers bazaar. Business is conducted on thick, white mattresses with bolsters to lean against in typical Indian style. Weavers from Varanasi and adjoining areas come with their wares and sell them straight to shopkeepers and retailers. The weaver may have for sale just one sari on which he has lavished all his time and skill or a dozen saris that the whole family have woven together with the skill handed down the centuries. The bazaar is held for just a few hours every day. At satti bazaar you can get a Benarsi sari at a bargain.

KASHMIRI CARPETS are famous the world over. You can contact the tourist office and ask them to arrange a visit to the carpet factory where you can watch adults and children putting knot upon knot, making exquisite, thick carpets.

GET AWAY FROM IT ALL by renting a houseboat on Dal or Nagin Lake, Srinagar. The three to four roomed suites have running hot and cold water and large flowered terraces for sunbathing and evening cocktails. They are electrified, well-furnished and can be moved in and outside Srinagar for a separate fee. Each houseboat has a *shikara* boat attached to it. The cost varies from Rs 325 for a deluxe double room to Rs 65 for a single in a C-class houseboat.

LIVE LIKE A KING. At the Shiv Niwas Palace on top of the hill overlooking the lake city of Udaipur it's possible to live like a prince of yesteryears. You can be king for a night paying just RS 2,000 or US$125.

Shiv Niwas Palace is one of the half a dozen palace hotels of India. But unlike in other palaces the Maharaja Kumar of Udaipur still lives in a part of this palace. Three of the suites are regal and exclusive. Two of them have been furnished in the finest cut glass. Everything in the suites and that includes the sofas, the beds and the chandeliers are in Czechoslovakian cut glass. While one of the suites is in cool white cut glass, the other is in wine

red. The third equally extravagant suite is in silver. The suites open into a large courtyard with an oval-shaped swimming pool that looks more like a huge princely bathtub.

RIVER RAFTING. For those seeking adventure there is nothing quite as thrilling as rafting down one of India's four navigable rivers — the Ganga, Bhagirath, Alaknanda and the Beas.

The rafting season is from January to May and again from October to December. Though the Ganga is the holiest river of India and a dip in it is supposed to be cleansing and purifying, it is also a "fun river" and much of the rafting is down this river. But more exhilarating than rafting down the Ganga is a trip down the Bhagirath. The many rapids and rocks that the boats have to negotiate through make the journey more exciting. The Alaknanda and the Beas, like the Ganga, are calmer rivers and easier to navigate. A trip can last for two days or more.

Those interested in river rafting should write to the Indian River Rafting Company at least a month in advance. Address: Indian River Rafting Company, 606 Akashdeep Building, Barakhamba Road, New Delhi. Tel: 3312773.

CAMEL SAFARIS. There is a unique kind of beauty and majesty in the sand dunes and rugged landscape of the desert terrain of Rajasthan. For those seeking adventure the best way to capture the spirit of this desert country and to cover its uninhabited expanses is to take a camel safari.

About a dozen safari routes have been worked out so that you can see different aspects of Rajasthan — like the tribal life, the beautiful, Shekhawati *havelis* of Sikar district, the rat temple at Deshnokh or desert life with glimpses of the Great Indian Bustard and the graceful black buck or chinkara.

The safari season begins in October and ends in March before summer sets in. Each trek takes anything from four to 12 days but the programme is flexible so that you can divert from the beaten track or stay back at a camp if you chose to.

A camel safari cost Rs 450 per day and this includes the camels, tents, equipment, food, sleeping bags and mattresses. There are weekly departures from Delhi. Those interested should write to: World Expeditions, Address: B/412 Som Datt Chambers-1, 5 Bhikaji Cama Place, New Delhi, Tel. 607362.

EATING OUT in India is something of a culinary adventure. An almost unimaginable variety of cuisines can be found here and you can sample

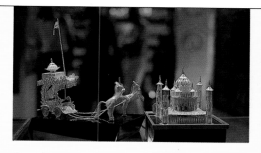

these in most major cities like Delhi, Bombay, Calcutta and Madras. Below are some suggested eating places in these four main capitals.

Delhi. Food from most parts of India can be tasted in Delhi. Apart from the excellent fare offered in the Indian, Western and Chinese restaurants of five-starred hotels there are several moderately priced eating houses where you get the local flavors and spices.

Mughal food is excellent in old Delhi and the walled city of Shah Jahan. Those with a good digestive system could try Karim's at Jama Masjid. The food is excellent and the atmosphere exotic with bearded patriarchs of the Muslim community, students and laborers at an adjoining table. Jawahar, Moti Mahal and Flora, also in this area, specialize in Mughlai food. You can have a good meal at these restaurants for Rs 50 to 60 per head.

In South Delhi, Moets is very popular with a restaurant and take-home facilities. In Malviya Nagar in South Delhi, Chic Fish, a wayside eatery is famous for its reasonably priced, barbecued kebabs and minced meat. Chicken and mutton *tikkas*, also made of minced meat and roasted on burning coal is another favorite Mughlai dish.

Woodlands in Lodhi Hotel, Dasaprakash in Ambassador Hotel, Bhaja Govindam on Asaf Ali Road and in the Defence Colony market offer excellent south Indian food at reasonable rates. Coconut Grove restaurant in Yatri Niwas offers the specialities of Kerala, garnished and cooked in fresh coconut milk.

Low budget foreign travelers as well as the local people, particularly students, love the Nirulas fast food chain of restaurants in Connaught Place, under the Defence Colony flyover, at Chanakya cinema and near Jawaharlal Nehru University. The Indian version of McDonald's, Nirulas serves an appetizing range of salads, pizza, burgers and several Indian dishes too. The salad parlor is popular with those dieting or steering clear of spicy Indian food. You can eat as much salad and as many helpings as you want for a nominal Rs 38. Nirulas ice creams are undoubtedly among the best in the world and come in over 20 flavors.

Bombay. A gourmet's paradise all kinds of food are available in this city, from vegetarian *thalis* to Italian and French cuisine. Samovar restaurant in Jehangir Art Gallery is well worth a visit for this is where the artists of the city, the up-and-coming film stars and students meet. There is a set menu for lunch and chilled beer is available. Sheetal restaurant in the suburbs of Khar offers fresh

seafood. There are tanks full of crabs, prawns and live fish which the customers select from and it is cooked the way they want it. At Supper Club, the rooftop restaurant at Oberoi Towers, the food is excellent and you get an excellent view of the curve of Marine Drive with a myriad lights twinkling on the Queen's Necklace. Hotel Ambassador has a revolving restaurant called "The Top" from which you can see different areas of the city. The Shamiana at Taj Hotel is a 24-hour coffee shop where you are sure to meet everyone worth knowing in the city.

Calcutta. The only Indian city with a Chinatown, Calcutta is famous for its excellent Chinese restaurants. Among those recommended are Jade Garden, Park Hotel and Ming Room on Park Street, Barbeque also on Park Street and Kaan and Jimmy's Kitchen on Lower Circular Road.

To taste the special Bengali dishes, particularly fish, visit Suruchi at Elliot Road run by the All Bengal Women's Union Home. Shellfish baked inside tender coconut, steamed mustard fish and fish in rich yogurt sauce are excellent. A special fish lunch is priced at just Rs 20.

Calcutta has some excellent western-style restaurants on Park Avenue including Mocamba, Kwality, Trincas, Blue Fox and Skyroom. Live band music and dancing are added attraction.

Kathi kababs, meat rolled in flaky *parathas* or bread are another speciality of the city and excelling in this Muslim preparation is Nizam's, near New Market.

Madras. To really get the flavor of the south — if you can, turn vegetarian. South Indian food is completely different from north Indian food. It is not as greasy as north Indian food, may be chili hot but not as spicy as north Indian cuisine and there is an amazing variety of rice dishes. Rice is the staple diet of south India. Among the more popular rice dishes are lemon rice, coconut rice, tamarind rice, curd rice and *vangibhaat* (rice with fried brinjals). But it is the snacks or "tiffins" of the south — like *dosas*, paper thin pancakes stuffed with vegetable, *idly*, a soft paste of rice and lentils that is steamed and served with coconut chutney and sambar, and *vadas* — that are now available all over India and even in Indian restaurants abroad.

For a good vegetarian meal visit Hotel Connemara and Yamuna Vegetarian Restaurant on Mount Road. For nonvegetarian food, you can go to the Mahal Restaurant for tandoori dishes, the Golden Dragon in Taj Coromandel for Chinese food and Taco Tavern for Mexican.

Travel Notes

Land And People
With the lofty, snow-clad Himalayas serving as its northern border, India extends southwards some 3,200 kilometers across the Gangetic plains and the peninsular plateau which dips to the shores of the vast Indian Ocean. It is bounded by Burma and Bangladesh on its east, China and Nepal on its north and northeast and Pakistan on its northwest.

From west to east, from the small town Kori Kreek in the Rann of Kutch near the Pakistan border to the frontier town of Kanhan near Burma it is 3,000 kilometers more. The vast size of this country has given it a rich and diverse landscape. It is a fascinating conglomeration of deserts, tropical rainforests and alpine meadows.

The federal structure of the country divides it into 25 states and six union territories. The states of India can be compared with the countries of Europe — they are vast, have a sizable population and each state speaks a different language. The state of Rajasthan is nearly as large as France. Despite the many languages and dialects, English and Hindi serve as link languages. Hindi is primarily a language of north India, also known as the Hindi belt. In the south there are four main languages — Telugu, Tamil, Kannada and Malayalam. All these languages — except Tamil which is purely Dravidian — have their roots in Sanskrit which like Latin, has almost died out.

Hinduism, the dominant religion, is practiced by 83 per cent of the population, followed by Islam by 11 per cent. India is also the home of Christianity, Buddhism, Jainism and Sikhism.

India has a burgeoning population of about 850 million. Seventy per cent of this massive population, however, still lives in villages. As in all developing countries there is a fascination for the big cities and a constant trek to them for jobs and quick money. Calcutta and Bombay rank among the most populated cities of the world. Delhi has the third largest population in India while Madras is the fourth largest city of India.

How To Get There
You can enter India by air, sea or overland through Afghanistan and Pakistan. Overland travel, however, is not advisable because of the trouble in Iran, Iraq and till very recently in Afghanistan.

Most visitors to India arrive by air at one of its four major international airports — Indira Gandhi International (Delhi), Sahar (Bombay), Dum Dum (Calcutta) and Meenambakam (Madras). More than 50 international airlines operate flights to India.

Although cruise ships do not come to India on a regular basis, several do call at Bombay, Calcutta and Madras periodically.

When To Go
The best time to visit India is from October to March when it is pleasant and cool, with bright sunny days. Those seeking to visit the towns in the plains of India should avoid venturing out in the summer months, particularly May and June when it gets extremely hot with temperature rising up to 45 to 50 degrees centigrade. However this would be an opportune time to visit hill resorts like Srinagar, Simla or Kulu Manali as they provide cool retreats during the hot summer months. You can go mountaineering or trekking. Towards the end of May the wet season begins when the southwest monsoon breaks out on the west coast and moves across the rest of the country through June and July. During this period, most of India experiences heavy rainfall, especially northeast India. Travel may be uncomfortable but not impossible.

Entry and Customs Rules
All foreigners except Nepalese or Bhutanese require visas for entry into India. Three kinds of visa are issued by the Indian government: tourist, entry and transit. Tourist visas are valid for three months and tourists must arrive within six months from the date of issue. Entry visas apply to those coming in for business, employment or permanent residence. Transit visas are issued to persons passing through India on transit to another destination and is valid only for 15 days. Applications for extension of visa can be made at the Foreigners Registration Offices at major cities like New Delhi, Bombay, Calcutta and Madras.

Special permission are required for visits to the following areas: Assam, Andaman and Nicobar Islands, Punjab, Darjeeling and Meghalaya, Tripura, Sikkim and the northern districts of West Bengal. Requests to visit these places should be made to the Indian Embassy in the home country at least six weeks in advance.

A Foreign Travel Tax of Rs 300 is levied on passengers embarking on journeys to any destination outside India. For journeys to neighboring countries like Pakistan, Bangladesh, Burma, Sri Lanka, Nepal and the Maldives the levy is Rs 100.

There are no restrictions on the amount of foreign currency or traveler's checks into India provided a declaration is made by the visitor in the Currency Declaration Form on arrival. This will not only facilitate exchange of currency but also

reconversion of unspent rupees later when leaving the country. The visitor is advised to keep all receipts of currency exchange transactions. Cash, bank notes and travelers' checks up to US$1,000 need not be declared at the time of entry. With the exception of rupee traveler's checks, no Indian currency whatsoever can be brought in or taken out of the country.

Visitors are allowed to bring in 200 duty-free cigarettes or 50 cigars or 250 grams of tobacco and alcoholic liquor up to .95 liters. However certain goods are prohibited and these include the import of dangerous drugs, live plants, gold, gold coins, gold and silver bullion. So is the export of antiquities more than 100 years old and all animal products.

Getting Around In India

By Air

Equipped with a large and modern fleet Indian Airlines has the world's second largest domestic networks. It carries an amazing number of people to 61 destinations in the country and also flies to Afghanistan, Bangladesh, the Maldives, Nepal, Pakistan, Sri Lanka, Singapore and Thailand. But despite its facilities it is not easy to get around if the trip is not planned in advance.

The introduction of computers has simplified reservation and travel by air. Reservation for multi-sector itineraries is now possible from major Indian cities like Delhi, Calcutta, Bombay, Madras, Hyderabad and Bangalore. For travel in the peak season (October to March) advance reservation is advisable as flights are heavily booked.

Indian Airlines offers many great fares to experience the wonder that is India. Its Discover India Fare of US$400 permits unlimited travel within India for 21 days. The India Wonderfare allows unlimited travel in one of the north, south, east or west India regions for seven days for US$200. For US$300, Tour India permits any six flights anywhere in India within 14 days. And for those below 30 years there is a special Youth Fare which offers a savings of 25 per cent on US$ air fare on domestic and Indo-Nepal sectors.

A feeder airline to Indian Airlines, Vayudoot flies smaller aircrafts like Dornier and Fokkers to 90 smaller towns of India from fixed bases at Delhi, Bombay, Calcutta, Hyderabad and Bhopal.

By Rail

The Indian Railways are the largest rail network in Asia and the second largest in the world. Nearly 11,000 trains crisscross about 62,000 kilometers

of rail route, connecting some 7,000 railway stations. The most comfortable way of traveling the subcontinent by rail is by air-conditioned first class, two-tier air-conditioned sleeper and air-conditioned chair car. Travel by non-air-conditioned cars is not recommended because it could get hot and dusty. Since, as in the case of air travel, there is a heavy rush for rail travel, advance booking and reservation of journeys is advocated.

For those on extended tours of the country Indrail passes allow seven days of air-conditioned first class travel for US$190 and 90 days of travel in the same class for US$690. By air-conditioned chair car first class/AC sleeper the cost is only US$95 and US$345 for the same period. If you go by ordinary second class it will cost US$45 for seven days and US$150 for 90 days. The passes, which so far were sold only within India, can now be bought outside India through General Sales Agent appointed by the Indian Railways.

Food can usually be ordered through a coach attendant. Several trains have dining cars attached and cold drinks and snacks are served in the compartment.

By Bus

Almost the whole country is connected by bus. Though interstate buses are crowded, noisy and slow there are some deluxe air-conditioned express buses running an efficient service. All cities have interstate bus termini and bus seats can be reserved in advance. Bus travel within most cities however is arduous and not recommended.

A-Z General Information on India

Business Hours

Government offices function five days a week from 9 am to 5.30 pm. All government offices are closed over the weekend though shops, banks and other services function normally. Shops are normally open till 7.30 pm. Government shops like the Cottage Emporiums which cater to tourists however are closed on Sundays. Several busy shopping centers, however stay open on Sunday and close one day of the week. Banks are open for public dealing from 10 am to 2 pm, Monday to Friday and Saturdays, from 10 am to 12 noon. The Ashok Hotel in New Delhi has a bank that is open 24 hours for money changing.

Clothing

During the summer season loose cottons and sandals or the Indian *chappal* (slippers) are ideal. These can be bought in India at reasonable prices.

In winter, a couple of sweaters as well as a jacket is needed especially in the north where the night temperatures can drop dramatically. In the day when it is still bright and sunny a lightweight sweater will suffice. For footwear in winter a comfortable pair of sneakers is recommended.

Currency

Indian currency is based on the decimal system with each Indian rupee consisting of 100 paise. Coins are in denominations of 20, 25, 50 paise, one rupee and two rupees. Paper notes are in denominations of 1, 2, 5, 10, 20, 100, 500. The exchange rate is roughly Rs 16 to US$1.

Electricity

Power is 220 volts at 50 Hz. Adapters are available in larger hotels to provide voltage suited to your electrical appliances.

Festivals and Holidays

Festivals are an intrinsic part of the Indian way of life. Most Indian festivals follow the lunar month, so the dates vary from year to year. Only the dates of fixed holidays are provided in the listing below.

January/February

Makara Sankranti/Pongal — Indian harvest festival celebrated in south India and parts of northern India. It is an exuberant three-day festival.

Republic Day (January 26) — A public holiday commemorating the declaration of India as a republic in 1950. Parades are held in all state capitals and are at their most spectacular in New Delhi.

Vasant Panchami/Shri Panchami — Spring festival honoring Saraswati, the Goddess of Learning. Books, pens and other instruments of learning are placed at her shrine.

Holi — This lively festival of colors heralding the advent of spring is celebrated by the throwing of colored powder and water.

Shivaratri — This festival is devoted to the worship of Shiva, one of the most powerful deities of the Hindu pantheon.

March/April

Good Friday — A public holiday marking the crucifixion of Christ.

Gangaur — Essentially a festival for women and girls this Rajasthani spring festival honors Parvati, the consort of Shiva.

Baisakhi — Celebrated in northern India, this festival marks the beginning of the Hindu solar new year. It is of special significance to the Sikhs as it was on this day some 500 years ago that Guru Gobind Singh converted them into a martial race.

Ram Navami — Marks the birth of Lord Rama, an incarnation of Vishnu. Devotees chant prayers and sing ballads.

Mahavir Jayanti — A public holiday celebrating the birth of the 24th and last Jain tirthankara. Pilgrims gather at Jain temples and shrines all over the country.

May/June

Id-ul-Fitr (Ramzan-Id) — A public holiday it marks the end of Ramzan, a month of fasting for Muslims. It is celebrated amidst much rejoicing and feasting.

Buddha Purnima — A public holiday celebrating the birth, enlightenment and attainment of Nirvana of Buddha.

Rath Yatra (Car festival) — A spectacular temple-festival in Puri, Orissa. Huge chariots are taken out in honor of Lord Jagannath.

July/August

Id-ul-Zuha (Bakr-Id) — Muslim festival commemorating Prophet Ibrahim's sacrifice of his son in obedience to a command of God. It is a public holiday.

Teej — A Rajasthani festival which welcomes the advent of the monsoon. It is also the swing festival dedicated to the Goddess Parvati, the consort of Lord Shiva.

Naga Panchami — Festival in which the cobra is worshiped in the form of Sesha, the thousand-hooded serpent.

Independence Day (August 15) — A public holiday celebrating India's independence.

Raksha Bandhan — Celebrated mainly in northern and western India. Sisters tie silken, colorful *rakhis* (amulets) around their brothers' wrists and pledge their love for each other.

Janmasthami — Anniversary of Lord Krishna's birth. Ceremonies and prayers are conducted at temples dedicated to the god.

September/October

Ganesh/Vinayak Chaturthi — Clay models of Ganesh, the auspicious elephant-faced god, are worshiped and taken out in grand processions to be immersed in the sea or a lake.

Onam — Kerala's harvest festival and a time for feasting and fun.

Gandhi Jayanti (October 2) — Mahatma Gandhi's birth anniversary. A public holiday.

Dussehra/Durga Puja — Celebrated with great pomp, this festival commemorates the victory of Lord Rama, in the epic *Ramayana*, over Ravana — the triumph of good over evil. The most popu-

lar of all Indian festivals, it runs for 10 days. It is a two-day public holiday.

Diwali — The gayest of all Indian festivals this Festival of Lights celebrates the return of Lord Rama after 14 years of exile..Fireworks and crackers add color and noise to the celebrations.

November/December

Pushkar Fair — Huge cattle market and camel fair at Pushkar, Rajasthan, where the celebrations include colorful camel races.

Guru Nanak Jayanti — Sikhs celebrate the birth anniversary of Guru Nanak, the founder of Sikhism. A public holiday.

Christmas — Anniversary of Jesus Christ' birth. A public holiday.

Health And Medical Care

A valid international certificate of vaccination for yellow fever is required for visitors from yellow-fever infected areas. No other vaccination certificate is required for entry into India but visitors are advised to have cholera, typhoid, hepatitis and tentanus shots before coming to India.

Come prepared with your own medicines for common ailments like diarrhoea for which you are advised to bring some proprietary medication such as Lomotil. Carry anti-malaria tablets as a precaution against malaria. Avoid drinking unboiled water — stick to the bottled or packaged drinks, taken without ice. Take fruit which has skin that can be peeled off and try to avoid salads except in recommended hotels and eating places. Rabies has a high occurrence rate here, so if bitten by a dog or a monkey the necessary course of injection should be taken.

Hotels And Accommodation

There is a range of hotels and accommodation to suit every kind of budget. In the deluxe and first-class hotels the accommodation is of high international standard. There is usually a choice of Indian, Western and Chinese cooking. Often the hotels are situated in extensive gardens and many have swimming pools, health club and other facilities like shops, bars, travel counter and even a resident fortune-teller. The standard of restaurants in the top hotels is excellent for a wide variety of food and some hotels have food festivals where you can taste the fare of different regions of India.

Bookings should be done well in advance — at least two to three months — for in the peak season from October to March hotels fill up extremely fast, especially in Delhi.

Valuables should be put in a safe deposit vault in the hotel or guest house and a receipt procured.

Remember also that there is a 10 per cent surcharge on room rents and on all food and beverages consumed in a hotel.

Though air-conditioned rooms are available in most big cities and big league hotels, in smaller towns the rooms have desert coolers in place of air-conditioners. These emit a blast of cooled air and are quite effective in April, May and June before the monsoon sets in.

Under the title of Ashok, the government Indian Tourist Development Corporation (ITDC) operates a chain of neat, clean and efficient hotels in all big cities of India. Hotel Ashok in Delhi, a grand, rambling building which plays host to most international conferences organised by the government, has its highest tarrifs in Delhi. Single room is Rs 1,250, executive suite is Rs 2,000 and deluxe suite is Rs 7,000 for a night. In smaller towns like Aurangabad the maximun for a double bedroom is Rs 595.

The Taj group has some of India's most regal hotels including the luxurious Taj Mahal Intercontinental in Bombay, the romantic Rambagh Palace in Jaipur, Lake Palace in Udaipur and the magnificent Fort Aguada resort in Goa.

The Oberoi, the Welcomgroup, the Clarks, the Air India associated Centaur chain and Hyatt Regency are among the other popular but luxurious hotel chain in India.

The following is a handpicked list of accommodation choices in prime tourist areas.

Deluxe and First Class
Delhi
Ashok Hotel, 50-B Chanakyapuri, Tel. 600121, 600412

Hotel Oberoi New Delhi, Dr Zakir Hussain Marg, Tel. 363030

Hotel Maurya Sheraton, Diplomatic Enclave, Tel. 3010101

Taj Palace Inter Continental, Diplomatic Enclave, Tel. 3010404

The Taj Mahal Hotel, I Man Singh Rd, Tel. 3016162

Hyatt Regency Delhi, Bhikaiji Cama Place, Tel. 609911

Claridges Hotel, 12 Aurangzeb Rd, Tel. 3010211

Hotel Imperial, Janpath, Tel. 3325332

Agra
Hotel Mughal Sheraton, Fatehabad Rd, Tel. 64701

Hotel Agra Ashok, The Mall, Tel. 76223-27

Varanasi
Hotel Taj Ganges, Nadesar Palace Grands, Tel. 42480
Hotel Clarks Varanasi, The Mall, 42401-6

Jaipur
Rambagh Palace Hotel, Bhawani Singh Rd, Tel. 75141
Hotel Clarks Amer, Jawaharlal Nehru Marg, Tel. 822616

Srinagar
Oberoi Palace, Gupkar Rd, Tel. 75751-2
Centaur Lake View Hotel, Dal Lake, Tel. 75667
Hotel Broadway, Maulana Azad Rd, Tel. 79101-2

Bombay
The Oberoi Towers, Nariman Point, Tel. 2024343
Taj Mahal Intercontinental, Apollo Bunder, Tel. 2023366
Welcomgroup Searock Sheraton, Land End, Tel. 6425454
Hotel President, 90 Cuffe Parade, Tel. 4950808
Holiday Inn, Juhu Beach, Tel. 6204444
Ambassor Hotel, Nariman Rd, Tel. 2041131

Goa
Majorda Beach Resort, Majorda, Tel. 20751
Oberoi Bogmalo Beach, Bogmalo, Tel. 2191
Cidade De Goa, Vainguinim Beach, Dona Paula, Tel. 3301-7
Fort Aguada Beach Resort, Sinquerim, Tel. 750107
Taj Holiday Village, Sinquerim, Tel. 7514-17

Aurangabad
Welcomgroup Rama International, R-3 Chikalthana, Tel. 82455
Ajanta Ambassador Hotel, Chikalthana, Tel. 8211

Udaipur
Lake Palace Hotel, Pichola Lake, Tel. 23241-5
Shivnivas Palace, Pichola Lake, Tel. 28239
Laxmi Vilas Palace Hotel, between Pichola and Fatehsagar Lakes, Tel. 24411-13

Khajuraho
Hotel Chandela, Tel. 54, 94-95
Hotel Jass Oberoi, Bye Pass Rd, Tel. 66, 85

Calcutta
The Oberoi Grand, 15 Jawaharlal Nehru Rd, Tel. 292323
Hotel Airport Ashok, Calcutta Airport, Tel. 575111
Park Hotel, 17 Park St, Tel. 297336

Madras
Taj Coromondel Hotel, 17 Nungambakkam High Rd, Tel. 474849

Welcomgroup Chola Sheraton, 10 Cathedral Rd, Tel. 473347
Welcomgroup Park Sheraton, 132 TTK Rd, Tel. 452525

Bangalore
Welcomgroup Windsor Manor Sheraton, 25 Sankey Rd, Tel. 79431
Hotel Westend, Race Course Rd, Tel. 29281

Mysore
Lalitha Mahal Palace Hotel, Tel. 26316

Moderate
Delhi
Hotel Marina, G-59 Connaught Circus, Tel. 3324658
Nirula's Hotel, L-Block, Connaught Place, Tel. 3322419
Hotel Ambassador, Sujjan Singh Park, Tel. 690391
Hotel Alka, 16/90, Connaught Circus, Tel. 344328
Hotel President, 4/23-B Asaf Ali Rd, Tel. 277836
Ranjit Hotel, Ranjit Singh Rd, Tel. 266001
Hotel Janpath, Janpath, Tel. 3320070
York Hotel, K-Block, Connaught Circus, Tel. 3323769
Hotel Broadway, 4/15 Asaf Ali Rd, Tel 273821
Hotel Diplomat, 9 Sardar Patel Rd, Tel. 3010204

Agra
Hotel Clarks Shiraz, 54 Taj Rd, Tel. 72421
Hotel Galaxy Ashok, Taj Ganj, Tel. 64171
Hotel Mumtaz, 181/2 Fatehabad Rd, Tel. 64771-6

Varanasi
Hotel de Paris, The Mall, Tel. 43582
Hotel Diamond, Bhelupura, Tel. 56561
Hotel Varanasi Ashok, The Mall, Tel. 42551

Jaipur
Hotel Arya Niwas, Sansar Chandra Rd, Tel. 73456
Bissau Palace, near Chandpol Gate, Tel.74191
Hotel Khasa Kothi, MI Rd, Tel. 75151
Jaipur Emerald Hotel, Mirza Ismail Rd, Tel. 78682
Mansingh, Sansar Chandra Rd, Tel. 78771

Bharatpur
ITDC Bharatpur Forest Lodge, Tel. 2260

Sariska
Hotel Sariska Palace

Jaisalmer
Narayan Niwas Palace, Tel. 2408

Srinagar
Hotel Parimahal, Dal Lake, Tel. 71235
Nedou's Hotel, Hotel Rd, Tel. 73015-6

Hotel Pamposh, Residency Rd, Tel. 75601-2
Hotel Zabarvan, Boulevard Rd, Tel. 71441-2
Welcomgroup Gurkha Houseboats, Tel. 75229

Ladakh
Shambala Hotel, Leh, Tel. 67
Welcomgroup Highlands, Kargil, Tel. 41

Bombay
Ritz Hotel, Nariman Rd, Tel. 220141
Hotel Apollo, 22 Landsdowne Rd, Tel. 2020223
Ascot Hotel, 38 Garden Rd, Tel. 240020
Grand Hotel, 17 Sprott Rd, Tel. 268211
Sun-n-Sand, 39 Juhu Beach, Tel. 6201811
Hotel Godwin, 41 Garden Rd, Tel 241226

Goa
Hotel Fidalgo, 18 June Rd, Panjim, Tel. 6291
Hotel Mandovi, Bandodkar Marg, Tel. 6270
Keni's Hotel, 18 June Rd, Panjim, Tel. 4581

Aurangabad
Hotel Aurangabad Ashok, Dr Rajendra Prasad
  Marg, Tel. 4520
Hotel Amarpreet, Nehru Marg, Tel. 4615

Udaipur
Hotel Shikarbadi, Ahmedabad Rd, Tel. 25321
Hotel Lakend, Alka Puri, Fatehsagar Lake,
  Tel. 23841
Hotel Anand Bhawan, Fatehsagar Rd, Tel. 23256

Khajuraho
Hotel Khajuraho Ashok, Tel. 24
Hotel Payal, Tel. 76

Calcutta
Hotel Hindustan International, 235/1 Jagadish
  Chandra Bose Rd, Tel. 442394
Great Eastern Hotel, 1-3 Old Court House,
  Tel. 282331
Hotel New Kenilworth, 1-2 Little Russell St,
  Tel. 448394
Fairlawn Hotel, 13-A Sudder St, Tel. 244460
Lytton Hotel, 14 Sudder St, Tel. 291875

Darjeeling
Windamere Hotel, Observatory Hill, Tel. 2397
Tourist Lodge, The Mall, Tel. 2611

Bhubaneswar
Hotel Ashok Kalinga, Gautam Nagar, Tel. 53318
Hotel Konark, Tel. 53330

Puri
Southeastern Railway Hotel, Tel. 62
Hotel Vijaya International, Tel. 2701

Madras
Savera Hotel, 69 Dr Radhakrishnan Rd, Tel
  474700
Connemara Hotel, Binny Rd, Tel. 860123
Hotel Imperial, 14 Whannels Rd, Tel. 566176
Hotel President, Edward Elliots Rd, Tel. 842211
New Victoria Hotel, 3 Kennet Lane, Tel. 567738

Madurai
Hotel Madurai Ashok, Alagarkoil Rd, Tel. 42531
Pandyan Hotel, Alagarkoil Rd, Tel. 26671

Bangalore
Bangalore International, 2A-2B Crescent Rd, High
  Grounds, Tel. 258011-7
Hotel Harsha, 11 Venkataswamy Naidu Rd,
  Tel. 565566
Hotel Shilton, St Marks Rd, Tel. 568185

Mysore
Rajendra Vilas Palace, Chamundi Hills, Tel. 20690
Hotel Metropole, 5 Jhansi Lakshmi Bai Rd,
  Tel. 20681
Hotel Highway, New Bannimantap Extension-7,
  Tel. 21117

Inexpensive
Delhi
Hotel Metro, N-49, Connaught Circus,
  Tel. 3313856
Central Court Hotel, Connaught Circus,
  Tel. 3315013
Hotel Regal, S.P. Mukerjee Marg, Tel. 2526197
Hotel Flora, Dayanand Rd, Tel. 273634
YMCA Tourist Hotel, Jai Singh Rd, Tel. 311915

Agra
Lauries Hotel, Mahatma Gandhi, Tel. 77047
Hotel Amar, Fatehabad Rd, Tel. 65696

Varanasi
Pallavi International Hotel, Hathwa Market,
  Tel. 52263-4
Gautam Hotel, Ramkatora, Tel. 44015
Tourist Bungalow, Parade Kothi, Tel. 43413

Jaipur
Gangaur Tourist Bungalow, MI Rd, Tel. 60231
Teej Tourist Bungalow, Bani Park, Tel. 74206

Bharatpur
Saras Tourist Bungalow, Agra Rd, Tel. 2169

Pushkar
Sarovar Tourist Bungalow, Tel. 40

Chittorgarh
Panna Tourist Bungalow, Tel. 273

Jaisalmer
Moomal Tourist Bungalow, Tel. 2392
Jaisal Castle Hotel, Tel. 2362

Srinagar
Hotel Mazda, Boulevard Rd, Tel. 72842
Hotel Boulevard, Boulevard Rd, Tel. 77089
Hotel Sabena, Residency Rd, Tel. 78046

Ladakh
State Tourist Bungalow

Bombay
Sea Green Hotel, 145 Marine Drive, Tel. 222294
Hotel Apollo, M Bhushan Marg, Tel. 230223
Strand Hotel, Ramachandani Marg, Tel. 241624
Hotel Hiltop International, 43 Pockkanwala Rd, Tel. 4930860
Shalimar Hotel, August Kranti Marg, Tel. 8221311
Sea Palace Hotel, Ramachandani Rd, Tel. 241828

Goa
Hotel Baia Do Sol, Baga Beach, Tel. 84/85
Hotel Metropole, Margao-Goa, Tel. 21516
Hotel La Paz Gardens, Swatantra Path, Tel. 2121

Aurangabad
Aurangabad Hotel Raviraj, Dr Rajendra Prasad Marg, Tel. 3939

Udaipur
Hotel Fountain, Sukhadia Circle, Tel. 26646
Hotel Damanis, near Telegraph Office, Tel. 25675

Khajuraho
Hotel Rahil, Tel. 62
Tourist Bungalow, Tel. 64

Calcutta
Carlton Hotel, 2 Chowringhee Place, Tel. 233009
Lindsay Guest House & Hotel, 8-B Lindsay St, Tel. 248639
YMCA, 25 Chowringhee, Tel. 233504

Darjeeling
Tiger Hill Tourist Lodge, Tel. 2813

Bhubaneswar
Hoter Prachi, 6 Janpath, Tel. 52521

Puri
Hotel Samudra, Tel. 2705
Sea View Hotel, Marine Parade, Tel. 117

Konarak
ITDC Ashok Tourist Lodge, Tel. 23

Madras
Hotel Kanchi, 28 Commander-in-Chief Rd, Tel. 471100
Hotel Atlantic, 2 Montieth Rd, Tel 860422
Hotel Blue Diamond, Poonamallee High Rd, Tel. 665981
New Woodlands, 72-75, Dr Radhakrishnan Rd, Tel. 473111
Hotel Palmgrove, 5 Kodambakkam High Rd, Tel. 471881

Pondicherry
International Guest House, Gingy Salai St, Tel. 2200
Hotel Ellora, Cathedral St, Tel. 2111
Seaside Guest House, Tel. 6494

Chidambaram
Hotel Raja Raja, 162 West Car St.

Thanjavur
Hotel Tamil Nadu, Gandhiji Rd, Tel. 57
Ashok Traveler's Lodge, Tel. 613007

Madurai
Hotel Tamil Nadu, Tel. 42461

Bangalore
Hotel Rama, 40/2 Lavelle Rd, Tel. 573381-4
Hotel Luciya International, 6 OTC Rd, Tel. 224148
Berry's Hotel, 46/1 Church St, Tel. 573331

Mysore
Hotel Dasaprakesh, Gandhi Square, Tel. 24444
Hotel Siddhartha, 73/1 Guest House Rd, Tel. 26869

Sravanabelagola
KSTDC Tourist Home
SP Guest House

Belur & Habid
KSTDC Tourist Cottages

Hampi
Malligi Tourist Home, off Hampi Rd, Tel. 8377
Hotel Sandarshan, Station Rd, Tel. 8574

Media And Movies

There are a good number of English daily newspapers in India. Tabloid journalism has not yet caught on and the newspapers tend to be serious. *The Times of India, The Hindustan Times, The Indian Express, The Statesman, The Hindu* and *The Telegraph* are the most popular papers and one or the other can be picked up in the big towns and cities.

India has also a wide radio and television network. Both English and Hindi programmes can be seen and heard on these networks. Totally con-

trolled by the government the television has just one channel in most cities. In some of the bigger towns the second channel operates for a few hours every evening.

All cities have several cinema halls with most of them showing Hindi films but in the big cities there are at least one or two halls showing English movies.

Photography

Cameras and films are expensive in India, so don't forget to bring them along with you on your trip. Generally there are no restrictions on the taking of photographs in India but with certain exceptions such as inside most places of worship, the use of artificial lighting when taking pictures of protected monuments and in museums, for which you have to seek special permission from the Archeological Survey of India.

Taboos And Customs

Indians are a warm and hospitable people. The normal Indian form of greeting is to fold hands and say "namaste". It is not expected from foreigners but it is always appreciated.

Before entering religious places — temples, gurdwaras and mosques — shoes have to be removed. In some places, like the Taj at Agra overshoes are provided. Most temples and mosques allow people to enter with socks. Leather bags and shoes, however, are banned in temples. Photography is prohibited inside most places of worship, so special permission may be required.

At home, particularly in south India, meals are eaten with properly washed hands and if you are a guest remember to use your right hand for eating. Most homes in cities, however, have become westernized in their eating habits and the necessary cutlery is provided.

Time

Indian time is 5^1/$_2$ hours ahead of Greenwich Mean Time and 9^1/$_2$ hours ahead of American Eastern Standard Time.

Taxis

Taxis are available in large cities and fares are charged on a per kilometer basis. For out of town travel there is a per kilometer charge plus an overnight charge of Rs 85. In Delhi, Bombay, Calcutta, Madras and other major cities metered taxis as well as luxury cars are available on hire. Tourists, however, cannot hire a car without a driver.

Tours

Many of the city and out-of-city tours in India are arranged either by national or state government tourism corporations. Tourists who are not making their own travel arrangements can do so through any one of the Government approved travel agencies in India. A list of these can be obtained from the Government of India Tourist Offices.

Tourist Information Offices

Government of India Tourist Offices in India and overseas provide travel information and literature to all visitors. It is a useful place to get maps and the latest brochures on Indian destinations. Below is a list of tourist offices in various cities in India where you can obtain information and advice.

Agra: 191 The Mall. Tel. 72377/67959
Aurangabad: Krishna Vilas, Station Road, Tel. 4817
Bangalore: KFC Building, 48 Church Street, Tel. 579517
Bhubaneswar: B-21 Kalpana Area, Tel 54203
Bombay: 123 M Karve Road, Tel. 291585, 293144
Calcutta: Embassy, 4 Shakespeare Sarani, Tel. 441475, 443521, 441402
Jaipur: Khasa Kothi State Hotel, Tel. 72200
Khajuraho: Near Western Group Temples, Tel. 47
Madras: 154 Anna Salai, Tel. 88685, 88686
New Delhi: 88 Janpath, Tel. 320342, 320005, 320008, 320109, 320266
Panaji (Goa): Communidade Building, Church Square, Tel. 3412
Varanasi: 15-B The Mall, Tel. 43189.

Useful Vocabulary

English	Hindi
Hello./Goodbye.	*Namaste.*
Thank you.	*Dhanyavad.*
Speak slowly.	*Asta bolio.*
I don't understand.	*Main nahin samjha.*
Excuse me.	*Maph karna.*
How are you?	*Aap kaise hain?*
What time is it?	*Kya time hua?*
I don't know.	*Mai nahi janta hoon.*
yes, no	*haan* (n silent), *nahi*
today, tomorrow	*aaj, kal*
yesterday	*kal*
who, when, where	*kaun, kabh, kahan*
why, what, which	*kyan, kya, kaunsa*
tea, milk	*chai, dood*
sugar, salt	*chini, namak*
rice, bread	*chaawal, double roti*
left, right, straight	*baya, daya, sidhaa*
sick, medicine	*bimaar, dawai*
hot water, cold water	*garam pani, thanda pan*

Index